BLEACHED FAITH

BLEACHED FAITH

THE TRAGIC COST
WHEN RELIGION IS FORCED
INTO THE PUBLIC SQUARE

Steven Goldberg

STANFORD LAW BOOKS

An Imprint of Stanford University Press

Stanford, California

Stanford University Press
Stanford, California

© 2008 by the Board of Trustees of the Leland Stanford Junior
University. All rights reserved.

Printed in the United States of America on acid-free,
archival-quality paper

Library of Congress Cataloging-in-Publication Data

Goldberg, Steven, 1947-
  Bleached faith : the tragic cost when religion is forced into the public
square / Steven Goldberg.
    p. cm.
  Includes bibliographical references and index.
  ISBN 978-0-8047-5861-1 (cloth : alk. paper)
    1. Freedom of religion--United States. 2. Church and state--United
States. 3. Religion and law--United States. 4. Church and state. I.
Title.

KF4783.G65 2008
342.7308'52--dc22
                                              2007041139

Designed by Bruce Lundquist
Typeset at Stanford University Press in 10/15 Sabon

To Missy

Contents

Acknowledgments

I OWE A GREAT DEBT to the Georgetown University Law Center and its dean, T. Alexander Aleinikoff, for the research time, financial support, and, most important, the intellectual and collegial atmosphere that made this book possible. In formal and informal talks, my colleagues, particularly Lisa Heinzerling, Louis Michael Seidman, and Girardeau Spann, and my wife, Miriam Goldberg, offered equal measures of ideas and encouragement. My students never stopped asking hard questions.

The Georgetown Law Library staff, led by Jennifer Locke Davitt, provided vital research assistance throughout this project. During a research semester in Cambridge, Massachusetts, I benefited as well from the resources of the Andover-Harvard Theological Library at Harvard Divinity School, Langdell Library at Harvard Law School, and Hayden Memorial Library at the Massachusetts Institute of Technology.

My family knows that I can never thank them enough.

BLEACHED FAITH

CHAPTER I

Introduction

IN THE SUMMER OF 2000, the government of McCreary County, Kentucky, posted the following language in the county courthouse:

I the LORD thy God am a Jealous God, visiting the iniquity of the fathers upon the children unto the third and fourth generation of them that hate me.

This is a surprising sentiment for an overwhelmingly Christian government that had earlier described Jesus as the "Prince of Ethics." But the government was not really endorsing this biblical passage. They were posting it because it is part of the Ten Commandments.

The Ten Commandments contain important teachings and a good deal of wisdom. But those who would post the commandments in courthouses and public buildings around the country are not really interested in studying the passages in Exodus and Deuteronomy where the commandments appear. They are posting a symbol.

The Ten Commandments have become the Nike Swoosh of religion. They are a casualty of the war to push religion into the public square. This is a war where the victories are more dangerous than the defeats. When religion wins, the vague and confusing symbols that enter public view do not stir anyone's soul.

It is a sign of weakness—an admission that religion needs artificial life support—to push religious symbols into the smothering embrace of government. If the push succeeds, religion is weakened further when it is distorted to fit governmental desires. Public recognition of God has been a part of American political life from the beginning of our country, and that is not going to change. But in recent years, an effort to present religion as a set of clumsy symbols has caused more harm than good. In American culture today, religion is inevitably watered down or distorted beyond recognition when its symbols are forced into the public square. The courts sometimes require this distortion, but even when they do not, our political culture does. America is home to many faiths with divergent teachings and ardent followers, and to a society that protects those of every faith and those with none at all.

I am delighted to live in a diverse and open culture where no one faith can or should dominate public life. But my focus in this book is on a different point. If religion is to have any real impact in America—if it is to serve as a source of moral values in a materialistic, scientific culture—it must have real content. That content emerges in hearts, homes, houses of worship, and in the private sector, not in government bureaucracies.

We will begin by looking at the odd fate of the Ten Commandments in America. In an endless series of bitter and costly legal battles, courts have sometimes allowed the display of the Ten Commandments on public property and sometimes forbidden it. But the commandments have gotten lost in the process. Christians have lost sight of the Jewish origins of the commandments and of what Jesus said about which commandments really matter. Jews have forgotten that in the Jewish tradition, the Ten Commandments do not even apply to non-Jews. The Seven Commandments of Noah apply to the Gentile world, but reference to the Seven Commandments generally leads to blank stares.

Moreover, in those areas where the distinctive teachings of the Ten Commandments have been upheld by the United States Supreme Court, Christians and Jews alike have run away from those teachings. When Jehovah's Witnesses in the 1940s interpreted the commandments' ban on graven images to forbid them from pledging allegiance to the flag, voters reacted with fury. Only the Supreme Court protected the Witnesses.

Even more remarkable is the history of Sunday Closing Laws, which were inspired in large part by the Ten Commandments' call for Sabbath observance. In the decades after the Supreme Court's 1961 decision upholding those laws, legislatures, responding to the public's love of shopping, repealed virtually all of them. Today, whether your traditional Sabbath is Saturday or Sunday, you are likely to spend that day like every other day of the week. Apparently posting unread copies of the Ten Commandments in government hallways is more popular than following them.

We will turn next to the debate over teaching intelligent design in the public schools. Intelligent design has few supporters among mainstream scientists, a status it richly deserves. Courts have generally viewed it as a transparent effort to put Genesis in the classroom. But intelligent design poses a far greater threat to religion than it does to science or the law. The strange desire to depict God as a second-rate engineer has little resemblance to the teachings of any faith.

Intelligent design puts God in a witness protection program, speaking of an unnamed "intelligent agent" who limits himself to performing minor tasks, such as the construction of a bacterium's flagellum. By reducing the Almighty to "the God of the gaps," it removes religion from the realm of faith and values, the precise areas where science is inadequate.

Intelligent design, since it has to pretend to be science, is an unfaithful version of the more serious argument from design, a venerable religious argument that has inspired millions. Indeed, whether they believe in traditional religion or not, modern scientists from Einstein to superstring theorists express a faith in the order and beauty of the universe that puts advocates of intelligent design to shame. The faith of scientists should not be taught in a public school biology class any more than Genesis should be. But it is a telling commentary on the empty state of much modern religion today that there is more inspiration to be found in the science section of a bookstore than in the religion section.

Next we will turn to the remarkable saga of how Christmas and Chanukah have suffered in public life in America today. We will begin with the disputes over holiday displays on public property, where pitched courtroom battles are fought every December over the right to place crèches and Chanukah menorahs alongside Santa Claus and the Christmas tree. The only certainty in these cases is that to win the dubious honor of appearing on a city hall lawn, a holiday display has to be emptied of any real religious content. In one case, the public authorities chose to put a four-foot-tall plastic Frosty the Snowman in the holiday mix in a successful effort to pass judicial muster. Here, as with the Ten Commandments, a victory in court is a defeat for religion.

The current fate of these holidays in America is depressing. Chanukah, a minor celebration not mentioned in the Bible, has become the most public Jewish festival. The real story of Chanukah celebrates an effort by Jews to avoid assimilation, but because it falls near Christmas on the calendar, Chanukah has been entirely assimilated, complete with an imitation of Christmas gift giving.

The Chanukah menorah, a nine-branched candelabrum, has become a leading symbol of Judaism in America. Today, many Jews are puzzled when they see depictions of the ancient menorah fashioned by Moses and his followers in the desert, the menorah that is the oldest symbol in Jewish history. They are puzzled because the biblical menorah has seven branches. In modern American Judaism, Chanukah's symbols have replaced those of far greater meaning.

Christmas has suffered as well. For over a hundred years, Christians struggled with the commercialization of the holiday, as the birth of Jesus sometimes took second place to shopping sprees. But only in recent years have matters reached the point where prominent Christian spokespersons and religious groups have argued that Christmas is not commercial enough—it is now said to be vital that "Merry Christmas," not "Happy Holidays," be the slogan for profit-making stores. The law certainly permits Christmas to be a marketing tool in the private sector, but there was a time when this was resisted by Christians, not applauded. Caught between empty symbols in the public square and the profit motive in the aisles of Wal-Mart, the spiritual side of Christmas is being squeezed out of existence.

We will conclude with a survey of the legal and political environment in which battles over the Ten Commandments, intelligent design, and the public celebration of religious holidays take place. The message here is clear, and surprisingly uncontroversial. The freedom of religion we enjoy in the United States, both as a matter of law and practice, is extraordinary by any measure. We can practice our faith at home and in houses of worship, we have a constitutional right to private schooling that can be pervasively religious, and we can profess our beliefs and seek converts to an extent that we should never take for granted. If American religion becomes a watered-down broth that is indistinguishable from consumerism and science, we will have no one to blame but ourselves.

The strength of real religion in America today is not undercut by the limits on government-supported religion in public settings. The true power of religion flows from restricting the embrace of government while protecting free exercise. We are neither France, where secularism reigns supreme, nor Iran, where one faith rules the roost. In France, students in public school cannot wear the Muslim head scarf; in Iran, they must. In America, the American Civil Liberties Union and the religious right agree that every public school student has a right to wear religious garb if and only if he or she so desires.

We will look at what would happen if the American government were to turn the tables and require that every church post the Magna Carta on its walls or that Sunday School references to Jesus' teachings be accompanied by a disclaimer saying that the Gospels cannot explain "scientific proof" that love is simply a biochemical reaction. These tactics would be fruitless and counterproductive displays of insecurity that would undermine support for real political and scientific goals. It is hardly surprising that few bureaucrats or scientists favor such ridiculous measures. Yet this is exactly what religious leaders do. Their efforts to force their symbols into public buildings and to add their disclaimers to the teaching of evolution have precisely the embarrassing effect that no secular leader would ever seek.

I come to this enterprise as someone who stands outside the camps of the resolutely secular and the resolutely religious. Or perhaps I have a toe in each camp. My father was a physicist, and I have considerable respect for the explanatory power of science, although I do not believe it can tell us how to live our lives. I am a Jew who is not very observant, yet I have a strong Jewish identity. I confess that I have celebrated Chanukah with my family, including gift giving, more than I have celebrated most other Jewish holidays. But I do feel that I benefited from religious school and Hebrew instruction, and I have concluded from my reading in the Book of Job and elsewhere that religion can provide me with a sense of humility, faith, and values that science and secularism cannot.

I try in this book not to go beyond what I understand. In particular, I limit myself to the dangers to Christianity and Judaism caused by misguided policies because I simply lack the knowledge to discuss the many other faiths that are so important in modern America. I hope adherents of those faiths will speak out on how the issues raised here affect them. In the end, I do believe that, from where I stand, the danger to American religion comes not from its failure to be recognized in the public square but from the costs that come with that recognition.

I am certain of one thing. My opposition to pushing religion into the courthouse and the biology classroom does not stem from hostility to religion. I am opposed to bleached faith—the empty symbolism that diminishes the power of real belief.

CHAPTER 2

Erasing the Ten Commandments

THE TEN COMMANDMENTS have been around for well over three thousand years, and their remarkable teachings remain vital to those who read and care about the Bible. About thirty years ago, a concerted effort began to post edited, poorly translated versions of the commandments in public schools, courthouses, and other governmental settings. This movement has made considerable progress in just three decades in reducing the Ten Commandments to an empty symbol.

Led by the Family Research Council's "Hang Ten" movement and by politicians like Roy Moore, various legislatures and city councils have sought to post the Ten Commandments on public property.[1] The ostensible reason is that the commandments are the foundation of our legal code.[2] Narrow religious goals are often denied.[3] Although the commandments contain provisions ("Thou shalt not steal") that prefigure some of our laws, they also contain provisions ("Thou shalt not make unto thee any graven image") that are obviously religious. As a result, the commandments are sometimes posted next to a variety of secular legal texts, such as the Magna Carta.[4] In response, those who oppose posting the commandments have made various efforts to remove depictions of them from public settings.[5]

This modern movement on behalf of the Ten Commandments may be good politics. It may also, at times, succeed in the inevitable court battles, since the relevant United States Supreme Court precedents are not models of clarity. However, even though this movement may be good for some politicians, it is bad for religion. Winning the right to reduce the Ten Commandments to a supporting role in a secular civics lesson is not a victory for people of faith. It is the kind of victory that corrupts the victor. Opposing the movement to hang Ten Commandments plaques in government hallways does not reflect hostility to religion. It reflects respect for important religious teachings.

It has taken a great deal of effort to empty the Ten Commandments of any meaning. We will begin this remarkable story by looking at how the commandments are actually presented in the Bible. That will involve some very unfamiliar territory for many Americans, since the tablets Moses first brought down—the ones we call the Ten Commandments— often go unread, and the second set of tablets—the ones referred to in the Bible as the Ten Commandments—are almost entirely forgotten.

We will then turn to the modern understanding of the Ten Commandments among Christians, and we will see that they include highly controversial teachings. The controversy should not be surprising since the commandments appear in the Old Testament, where there are many rules that Christians do not follow. Moreover, even if one follows the commandments, their implications for practices like capital punishment have long been subject to debate.

Next we will look at the reception of the Ten Commandments in the American legal system. In 1980, the Supreme Court began to consider when and how the commandments can be posted in public buildings. Each of the Court's decisions has been 5–4, the results have varied, and the law in this area remains unsettled, to use a polite word. On the other hand, when we turn to Supreme Court decisions concerning efforts by Americans to follow the Ten Commandments, the Court has been re-markably supportive. The elected legislatures are the ones who have undermined those efforts to obey the commandments. In other words, if you believe that too few people are following the Ten Commandments, do not blame activist judges. Legislatures forced Jehovah's Witnesses to pledge to the flag despite the Witnesses' belief that this showed subser-vience to a graven image, and legislatures ended Sunday Closing Laws that supported Sabbath observance after the Supreme Court said such laws were constitutional. It appears that for many Americans, posting the Ten Commandments is more popular than obeying them.

In the end, if people of faith are unlucky and the movement to post the Ten Commandments succeeds, religion will suffer a costly blow. An important text in the Jewish and Christian traditions will have been watered down to an empty image.

THE TEN COMMANDMENTS
AS IF THE BIBLE MATTERED

The biblical laws that we know as the Ten Commandments first appear when God gives them to Moses on Mount Sinai. They appear (in Hebrew, of course) in Exodus 20:2–17. They are presented here as they appear in the King James translation of the Bible, with the verse numbers on the left. The King James translation has been found wanting in many respects by modern scholars,[6] and it is not followed by everyone—in particular, Jews and Catholics use other translations[7]—but it is the most familiar version to most Americans.

2 I am the LORD thy God, which have brought thee out of the land of Egypt, out of the house of bondage.

3 Thou shalt have no other gods before me.

4 Thou shalt not make unto thee any graven image, or any likeness of any thing that is in heaven above, or that is in the earth beneath, or that is in the water under the earth:

5 Thou shalt not bow down thyself to them, nor serve them: for I the LORD thy God am a jealous God, visiting the iniquity of the fathers upon the children unto the third and fourth generation of them that hate me;

6 And shewing mercy unto thousands of them that love me, and keep my commandments.

7 Thou shalt not take the name of the LORD thy God in vain; for the LORD will not hold him guiltless that taketh his name in vain.

8 Remember the sabbath day, to keep it holy.

9 Six days shalt thou labour, and do all thy work:

10 But the seventh day is the sabbath of the LORD thy God: in it thou shalt not do any work, thou, nor thy son, nor thy daughter, thy manservant, nor thy maidservant, nor thy cattle, nor thy stranger that is within thy gates:

11 For In Six Days The Lord Made Heaven And Earth, The Sea, And All

That In them is, and rested the seventh day: wherefore the LORD blessed the Sabbath day, and hallowed it.

12 Honour thy father and thy mother: that thy days may be long upon the land which the LORD thy God giveth thee.

13 Thou shalt not kill.

14 Thou shalt not commit adultery.

15 Thou shalt not steal.

16 Thou shalt not bear false witness against thy neighbour.

17 Thou shalt not covet thy neighbour's house, thou shalt not covet thy neighbour's wife, nor his manservant, nor his maidservant, nor his ox, nor his ass, nor any thing that is thy neighbour's.

The first thing that jumps out at the reader of this text is that there appear to be more than ten commandments here.[8] At this point in the Bible neither God nor Moses nor anyone else says there are ten, and they are not presented in a list of ten. Nonetheless, because later biblical passages refer to Ten Commandments (or Ten Statements, depending on the translation), it has been customary for both Jews and Christians to organize these sixteen verses into ten commandments.[9] This organization is achieved in a remarkable variety of ways. To give just one example, many Protestants treat "no other gods" (20:3) as the first commandment, and no "graven images," "thou shalt not bow down," and so on (20:4–6) as the second; whereas Catholics put those verses together as the first and, unlike the Protestants, separate into two commandments the prohibitions on coveting "thy neighbour's wife" and coveting "thy neighbour's" other goods (20:17).[10]

But, as noted previously, this numbering issue does not arise in the Bible itself. In fact, following Exodus 20 are eleven chapters filled with scores of commandments on a host of topics. Some of these are well known, at least in part:

Exodus 21

23 And if any mischief follow, then thou shalt give life for life,

24 Eye for eye, tooth for tooth, hand for hand, foot for foot,

25 Burning for burning, wound for wound, stripe for stripe.

26 And if a man smite the eye of his servant, or the eye of his maid, that it perish; he shall let him go free for his eye's sake.

Others are less well known. Many, for example, concern detailed specifications for the construction of the tabernacle, the portable sanctuary the Jews carried in the desert: "The length of one curtain shall be eight and twenty cubits, and the breadth of one curtain four cubits" (Exodus 26:2).

The narrative concerning Moses and Mount Sinai picks up in Exodus 32:19, where we learn that while Moses was on the mountain, the people below, growing impatient, built a golden calf and worshipped it. When Moses came down and saw this, his "anger waxed hot," and he threw down the tablets containing God's commandments and shattered them (32:19).

Soon thereafter, God commanded Moses to make two tablets of stone "like unto the first" and write upon these tablets "the words that were in the first" (34:1). On these new tablets Moses wrote "the words of the covenant, the ten commandments" (34:28). Thus, in Exodus, the phrase "ten commandments" refers to this second set of injunctions.[11] This is the set placed in the famous Ark of the Covenant, the sacred chest for holding the stone tablets that is kept in the tabernacle (40:20–21).[12]

These "ten commandments," which appear in Exodus 34:11–26, are quite different from the more famous first list. Although there is some overlap with the earlier enumeration ("Thou shalt worship no other god: for the LORD, whose name is Jealous, is a jealous God"; 34:14), there are also a set of detailed ritualistic requirements, such as, "The first of the firstfruits of thy land thou shalt bring unto the house of the LORD thy God," and "Thou shall not seethe a kid in his mother's milk" (26). Moreover, many of the best-known commandments in the first list, such as "Thou shall not commit adultery" and "Thou shalt not steal," do not appear in the second list. Nonetheless, it is clearly this second list that is referred to in the very next passage in Exodus: "And the LORD said unto Moses, Write thou these words; . . . And he wrote . . . the words of the covenant, the ten commandments" (27–28).

Some authorities refer to the first Ten Commandments, the familiar list, as the Ethical Decalogue and call the second set the Ritual Decalogue.[13] I will use the phrase "Ten Commandments" for the familiar first list because that is what "Ten Commandments" means to virtually everyone in our culture. And these famous Ten Commandments make a second appearance, albeit in altered form, in the Book of Deuteronomy, the fifth book of the Bible.[14] In Deuteronomy 4, Moses reminds the people that on Mount Sinai God "declared unto you his covenant, which he commanded you to perform, even ten commandments," which he wrote on stone (13). Then in the next chapter, Moses restates the famous list that we call the Ten Commandments (5:6–21).

This version of the Ten Commandments is quite similar to the version in Exodus 20, which I presented in full above. It has the same basic provisions. There are, however, a number of differences. For example, Exodus commands us: "Remember the Sabbath day, to keep it holy" (20:8), whereas Deuteronomy states: "Keep the Sabbath day to sanctify it, as the LORD thy God hath commanded thee" (5:12). To some, there is an important difference between "remembering" and "keeping."[15] The sense of difference concerning the Sabbath also appears in the differing justifications for Sabbath observance offered in the two versions of the Ten Commandments. In Exodus, Sabbath remembrance is commanded because the Lord made the world in six days and rested on the seventh (20:11). In Deuteronomy, by contrast, we observe the Sabbath because the Lord brought the people out of Egypt "through a mighty hand and by a stretched out arm: therefore the LORD thy God commanded thee to keep the Sabbath day" (5:15).

After Moses reminds the people of the Ten Commandments, he recalls how he broke the original tablets in anger at the golden calf (Deuteronomy 9:16–17) and how he later made a second set of the Ten Commandments, although at this point the contents of the second set are not repeated (10:1–5).

This, then, is the Bible's treatment of God giving the Ten Commandments to Moses and the people. There has been an enormous amount of writing, both by theologians and secular scholars, about the differences between the Exodus and Deuteronomy versions of the Ten Commandments, about the meaning of the Ritual Decalogue that appears on the second set of tablets, and so on.[16] For example, those writers who do not believe that the Bible is the word of God or that it was all written by Moses have attempted to identify when and by whom different passages may have been written.[17]

My concern is not to analyze these matters. It might be useful, however, to note that in the Jewish tradition, the Ten Commandments occupy a somewhat different role than many people realize, including both Jews and non-Jews. In the Jewish tradition, the first five books of the Bible—Genesis, Exodus, Leviticus, Numbers, and Deuteronomy—are the Torah, the most important source of Jewish law. To strictly observant Jews, the Torah contains 613 commandments, all of which must be obeyed.[18] For example, dietary rules, such as not eating pork, are set forth in the Torah (Leviticus 11:7–8). The Ten Commandments are important—they are sometimes viewed as a structure or set of categories into which other laws fit—but they are not to be given too much emphasis.[19] The point is that the Ten Commandments are not read apart from the rest of the Torah. For example, the commandment that the King James translation renders as "thou shalt not steal" is understood by Orthodox Jews to mean "thou shalt not kidnap," since theft of property is dealt with explicitly in another Torah passage, where it is treated as a tort, not a crime (see Exodus 22:1).[20] Moreover, in the Orthodox Jewish tradition, the Ten Commandments, like the various dietary and other rules, apply only to the Jewish people.[21] In this tradition, there is a different set of rules that God gave for all of humanity.

The Talmud, a set of commentaries on Jewish law, says that God gave Noah a set of seven laws that bind everyone, Jew and Gentile alike: Do not worship idols, do not murder, do not steal, do not be sexually immoral, do not blaspheme, do not eat the body of a living animal, and set up righteous and honest courts to apply fair justice.[22] I am not aware of any Jewish group that has called for posting these so-called

Noahide laws in public places, which is hardly surprising since many Jews, like many Christians, have been swept up in the idea that the Ten Commandments have a unique status.

THE MODERN MEANING OF THE
TEN COMMANDMENTS FOR CHRISTIANS

What do the Ten Commandments mean to Christians today? Because Christianity is the dominant American religion, the answer is crucial if we are to know what happens to religious teachings when the commandments are posted in courthouses and other public spaces. There is, of course, no one answer to the question. The many different Christian groups in modern America do not always agree on the role or meaning of the commandments. For some, biblical text is relevant primarily as metaphor, so the precise meaning of the Ten Commandments is not crucial. But even for the many Christians who do give weight to the text, the interpretation of the Ten Commandments varies quite a bit.

We begin with the question of the extent to which Jesus' teachings supplant the rules set forth in the Old Testament. Clearly, few Christians believe they are bound to follow the dietary rules set forth in the book of Leviticus. So what about the rules that appear in the Ten Commandments in Exodus and Deuteronomy? At times, Jesus referred to some of these rules.[23] For example, in Matthew we are told that Jesus said that "there is none good but one, that is, God: but if thou wilt enter into life, keep the commandments" (19:17). When asked "Which?" Jesus replied, "Thou shalt do no murder, Thou shalt not commit adultery, Thou shalt not steal, Thou shalt not bear false witness, Honour thy father and thy mother: and, Thou shalt love thy neighbour as thyself" (19:18–19). Here, Jesus is reiterating some, but not all, of the Ten Commandments, while adding the teaching to love thy neighbor as thyself, which does not appear in the Decalogue.

Elsewhere in Matthew, Jesus presents the following teaching about one of the Ten Commandments: "Ye have heard that it was said by them of old time, Thou shalt not commit adultery: But I say unto you, That whosoever looketh on a woman to lust after her hath committed adultery with her already in his heart" (5:27–28).

But these and other New Testament references to Old Testament teachings are understood by many Christians as best understood in light of Jesus' reply when challenged with the question, "Which is the great commandment in the law?" In answer, Jesus said, "Thou shalt love the Lord thy God with all thy heart, and with all thy soul, and with all thy mind. This is the first and great commandment. And the second is like unto it, Thou shalt love thy neighbour as thyself. On these two commandments hang all the law and the prophets" (Matthew 22:35–40).

These passages do not, of course, resolve the question of the role of the Ten Commandments in Christian belief. But they do suggest that the question is important. Let us explore a little further by looking at the status in Christian belief of three of the Ten Commandments: the ban on graven images, the question of Sabbath observance, and the edict "thou shalt not kill." We will continue to focus on those Christians who are deeply concerned with the meaning of biblical text.

As we have seen, the first commandments say in part, "Thou shalt have no other gods before me. Thou shall not make unto thee any graven image, or any likeness of any thing. . . . Thou shalt not bow down thyself to them, nor serve them." For many Christians, the key here is to avoid bowing down or worshipping a graven image. There is no problem with religious pictures or statues, so long as you are worshipping God, not the object.[24] But there are some Christians who take a different view. They oppose making or having graven images in a broad sense. In an extreme example, some devout Christians have challenged the requirement that they carry a photograph on their driver's license since they view the photo as a graven image.[25]

And the ban on "graven images" raises disagreements in more ordinary settings as well. There are questions of degree and of emphasis, as when some Protestants express unhappiness with the stained-glass windows they see in Catholic churches because of the Protestants' concern with graven images.[26] There are also important disputes about what constitutes an improper bowing down. For Jehovah's Witnesses, the flag is a graven image, and they will not salute it because they regard that as bowing down in violation of this commandment.[27]

Christians are also divided in their view of the rationale given in the Ten Commandments for the ban on other gods and graven images: "I the LORD . . . am a jealous God, visiting the iniquity of the fathers upon the children unto the third and fourth generation of them that hate me; and shewing mercy unto thousands of them that love me." Some Christians believe this literally. If you sin, your offspring will suffer for four generations as a result. God's mercy is shown by the fact that your loving him will benefit your descendants for thousands of generations.[28] Other Christians reject the idea that people will be made to suffer by God for something their great-grandfather did before they were born. They believe this teaching is changed in later portions of the Old Testament, or by the New Testament, or that it is, at most, a metaphor expressing God's power.[29]

Different interpretations of the Ten Commandments' requirement to "remember" (Exodus 20:8) or "keep" (Deuteronomy 5:12) the Sabbath are perhaps better known than the issues surrounding graven images. For most Christians this is a clear instance where the New Testament supersedes the Old. The Jewish Sabbath, Saturday, is replaced by Sunday, in memory of the Resurrection. Moreover, the Orthodox Jewish practice of strictly avoiding work and commerce of any kind on the Sabbath is not followed.[30]

But Christians do differ quite a bit on how Sunday should be observed. Is it enough to go to church and then right back to work and shopping, spending no time with your family? Obviously, not everyone is comfortable with that.[31] Moreover, some Christians, such as Seventh-Day Adventists, retain Sabbath observance on Saturday and adhere as well to a strict ban on work on that day.[32]

Finally, the different interpretations of the Ten Commandments statement "Thou shalt not kill" are perhaps the best known. Does this commandment, for example, forbid killing in self-defense?[33] Many discussions of this issue begin by noting that the King James translation may be misleading here. Many modern scholars translate the Hebrew as "Thou shalt not murder."[34] But the debates among Christians remain, and they are lively and important. Does this commandment, in light of Jesus' teachings in the New Testament, lead one to oppose capital punishment? Does it support pacifism? Does it concern abortion? Suffice it to say that there are a variety of Christian teachings on these vital matters.[35]

Noting the controversies about the meaning of the Ten Commandments is not meant to trivialize those commandments. Quite the contrary. If religion consisted of praising motherhood and apple pie, it would not be a very important social institution. It is precisely because the Ten Commandments are an influential text speaking to some of the most important and enduring human problems that we ought not treat them like an advertising slogan. The movement to post the Ten Commandments in schools, courtrooms, and other public places erases the commandments. Because the Ten Commandments appear in different versions in the Bible, are numbered and translated in different ways, are interpreted differently by different Christians, and are too long to fit neatly on a poster, the results of the movement are straight out of *Saturday Night Live*.

Consider the two Ten Commandment displays that came before the Supreme Court in 2005. We will look at this litigation and these displays in detail later. But a quick preview is enough to demonstrate the problem.

The posting in a McCreary County, Kentucky, courtroom included the language "I the LORD thy God *am* a jealous God, visiting the iniquity of the fathers upon the children unto the third and fourth generation," without even mentioning the following phrase about showing mercy for a thousand generations, let alone the fact that this teaching is not followed by many believers.[36] How many of those who supported the McCreary County posting believed they were liable for the sins of their great-grandfathers but not the sins of earlier ancestors?

Meanwhile, the Ten Commandments monument in Austin, Texas, has a neat, orderly list of *eleven* commandments.[37] It is true that the biblical passage in question contains sixteen verses, but everyone else in history has, one way or the other, grouped them into ten commandments. Only Texas managed to come up with eleven.

The displays in both Kentucky and Texas use the controversial translation "Thou shalt not kill" rather than "Thou shalt not murder."[38] Yet capital punishment is practiced in both Kentucky and Texas. Did those who supported these memorials take the trouble to actually read them?

THE SUPREME COURT AND
DISPLAY OF THE TEN COMMANDMENTS

The United States Supreme Court has rendered three decisions on efforts to display the Ten Commandments in the public square. Each has been a 5–4 judgment, and taken together, they make it hard to predict which displays are lawful and which are not. The Court decisions do illuminate the reality that even successful efforts to display the commandments do not further genuine religious goals.

The Supreme Court's involvement in the matter began when the Kentucky legislature, in 1978, passed a statute requiring the posting of a copy of the Ten Commandments in every public school classroom in the state.[39] The copies were to be purchased with private contributions. The statute did not say what version of the Ten Commandments would be posted, but it did state that "in small print below the last commandment shall appear a notation concerning the purpose of the display, as follows: 'The secular application of the Ten Commandments is clearly seen in its adoption as the fundamental legal code of Western Civilization and the Common Law of the United States.'"[40]

A challenge to the statute was promptly brought in state court by a group of plaintiffs, including a Quaker, a Unitarian, a nonbeliever, and a rabbi. A state trial judge upheld the statute, finding that its "avowed purpose" was "secular and not religious."[41] The Kentucky Supreme Court divided 3–3 on whether to affirm or reverse the trial court. Under Kentucky law, this meant that the trial court decision was affirmed. One of the Kentucky Supreme Court justices who would have struck down the statute noted that whatever "official" version of the Ten Commandments was finally chosen for posting, it would contradict the religious beliefs of some group.[42] As an example, he noted the dispute over whether the commandments ban "killing" or "murder."[43] He argued as well that some of the commandments, such as the ban on graven images, are purely religious and do not reflect the secular law of the United States.[44] One of the justices who would have upheld the display said that the Ten Commandments form the "basic tenets of a particular scheme of Western philosophical thought" rather than a religious teaching.[45]

In 1980, the United States Supreme Court, in the case of *Stone v. Graham*, struck down the Kentucky statute by a vote of 5–4.[46] The justices in the majority relied on previous decisions holding that a statute violates the non–Establishment Clause if it lacks a "secular legislative purpose."[47]

This test is easy to misunderstand. The First Amendment's ban on established religion does not mean that laws with a religious basis are unconstitutional. Every justice on the United States Supreme Court recognizes that a valid statute might be motivated in part by a religious purpose. For example, a legislator might vote to outlaw murder solely because he or she believes the Ten Commandments both ban murder and represent God's mandate. Yet the statute will be upheld because there are secular reasons for opposing murder. Another legislator might believe, for example, that a functioning economy and a fulfilling private life cannot be maintained in a society that allows murder.[48]

The Court's belief that a statute cannot have a *solely* religious purpose is not easy to enforce. How do you determine a legislature's purpose? Justices will often disagree on that question, and some justices believe the effort to figure out purpose is not worth the difficulties involved.[49] But to this day, in a variety of settings, a number of Supreme Court justices will strike down a statute if they believe its only motivation is religious.

We can imagine extreme cases where almost everyone will have at least some sympathy for this point of view. Suppose a town council in a heavily Catholic community required that a large crucifix, funded by private contributions, be placed in every public school classroom even though many students are not Catholic. Suppose further that all elected officials who voted for this statute said that they did so because of the "beauty of the crucifix and its influence on the art of Western civilization." These are secular purposes, but we would be forgiven, in this imaginary case, for doubting that they are the real purposes for the statute. One way or the other, most judges, of whatever religious background, are going to find that this imaginary statute constitutes an unconstitutional establishment of religion. If it is not, the legislature could, using the same "artistic" rationale, require that every public school teacher wear a crucifix or that every student do the same.

In *Stone v. Graham*, the majority of the Court believed that the Kentucky statute was not really based on the secular purpose stated in small print after the last commandment. They relied heavily on the fact that the commandments include purely religious teachings—such as "worshipping the Lord God alone [and] avoiding idolatry"—that could not be explained as part of "the legal code of Western Civilization and the Common Law of the United States."[50] Apparently, the majority thought the religious motivation of the Kentucky legislature was pretty obvious since the Court disposed of the case summarily in what is called a per curiam opinion.[51] This type of brief opinion not attributed to any single justice is generally used for easy cases.

The majority opinion in *Stone v. Graham* did not rule out all uses of the Ten Commandments in the public schools. The Court noted that the Bible "may constitutionally be used in an appropriate study of history, civilization, ethics, comparative religion, or the like."[52] They concluded that the posting of the commandments on the public school wall did not serve a valid function:

If the posted copies of the Ten Commandments are to have any effect at all, it will be to induce the schoolchildren to read, meditate upon, perhaps to venerate and obey, the Commandments. However desirable this might be as a matter of private devotion, it is not a permissible state objective under the Establishment Clause.[53]

Justice (later Chief Justice) Rehnquist wrote the primary dissent in *Stone v. Graham*. He would have accepted the statements of the Kentucky legislators and the finding of the trial judge that the posting of the commandments had the secular purpose of showing a link between the commandments and secular law. Rehnquist believed that "the religious nature of the first part of the Ten Commandments is beside the point. The document as a whole has had significant secular impact, and the Constitution does not require that Kentucky students see only an expurgated or redacted version."[54] More broadly, Justice Rehnquist argued that the idea that religion has to be kept strictly out of the public square is inconsistent with our history: "The Establishment Clause does not require that the public sector be insulated from all things which may have a religious significance or origin."[55]

Needless to say, the closely divided 1980 decision in *Stone v. Graham* did not resolve the question of whether the Ten Commandments could be displayed in public settings. First of all, *Stone* concerned public schools, where the Court, because of a concern with impressionable minors and mandatory attendance laws, is often more strict about the separation of church and state than they are in other public settings. In addition, both before and after *Stone* the Court has failed to agree on a consistent approach to Establishment Clause cases.[56] In the absence of clear precedents, the Court's decisions have been hard to predict.

In the years after *Stone*, litigation continued in the lower courts over various displays of the Ten Commandments. Finally, in 2005, the Supreme Court decided two cases on the subject on the same day. The cases had arisen in different states and involved different factual settings, but the Court took them up together, and many observers hoped the resulting decisions would clarify the law. Those hopes were not realized.

The first case concerned a monument erected on the grounds of the

Texas State Capitol in 1961.[57] The twenty-two acres surrounding the Capitol contain numerous monuments relating to themes such as the Heroes of the Alamo, Volunteer Firemen, Texas Cowboys, Pearl Harbor Veterans, and so on. The monument in question is six feet high and three and a half feet wide.

The history of how this Ten Commandments monument came to be on the grounds of the Texas State Capitol is remarkable. The Fraternal Order of the Eagles had donated paper copies of the commandments around the country. When Cecil B. DeMille, who was filming the movie *The Ten Commandments*, heard of the project, he stepped in and helped the Eagles donate granite monuments such as the one that ended up in Texas.[58]

The monument itself contains a rather odd collection of symbols and words. Above the text, we see an "eagle grasping the American flag, an eye inside of a pyramid, and two small tablets with what appears to be an ancient script. . . . Below the text are two Stars of David and the superimposed Greek letters Chi and Rho, which represent Christ [as well as] the inscription 'PRESENTED TO THE PEOPLE AND YOUTH OF TEXAS BY THE FRATERNAL ORDER OF EAGLES OF TEXAS 1961.'"[59]

The text itself is noteworthy as well. It reads as follows:

I AM the LORD thy God.

Thou shalt have no other gods before me.

Thou shalt not make to thyself any graven images.

Thou shalt not take the Name of the Lord thy God in vain.

Remember the Sabbath day, to keep it holy.

Honor they father and thy mother, that thy days may be long upon the land which the Lord thy God giveth thee.

Thou shalt not kill.

Thou shalt not commit adultery.

Thou shalt not steal.

Thou shalt not bear false witness against thy neighbor.

Thou shalt not covet thy neighbor's house.

Thou shalt not covet thy neighbor's wife, nor his manservant, nor his maidservant, nor his cattle, nor anything that is thy neighbor's.[60]

As we have seen, reconciling the sixteen verses in Exodus, which set forth the best-known biblical rendition of the commandments, with the statements in the Bible that "ten" commandments or statements were given to Moses and the people has led different religions to group the commandments differently. But throughout history every group has managed to come up with ten. The list above, as you can see, has *eleven* commandments, without even counting "I am the Lord thy God," which is the first commandment in the Jewish tradition.

Otherwise, the Texas monument is close to the King James translation from the Book of Exodus, using, for example, "thou shalt not kill," rather than "murder." Numerous passages from the King James translation, however, are left out, such as the mandate, "Six days shalt thou labour, and do all thy work: But the seventh day . . . thou shalt not do any work." And some are changed; for example, King James says thou shalt not covet thy neighbor's "ox, nor his ass," and the Texas version says "thou shalt not covet thy neighbor's . . . 'cattle.'"

In any event, this monument stood on state land for forty years without recorded protest, until, in 2001, Thomas Van Orden, a Texas resident who had encountered the monument for years while walking on the Capitol grounds, brought suit claiming that the display violated the Establishment Clause. The lower courts upheld the display, and the Supreme Court granted review.

The second Ten Commandments case considered by the Supreme Court in 2005 arose from a much more recent display.[61] In 1999, officials put up copies of the Ten Commandments in two county courthouses in Kentucky. A lawsuit was brought immediately, and over the next two years, the matter bounced between the county and the courts, which struck down an initial version of the display. At various points, county officials supported the display in a variety of ways, arguing, for example, that the Ten

Commandments are "the precedent legal code upon which the civil and criminal codes of . . . Kentucky are founded," noting that the Kentucky House of Representatives had referred to Jesus Christ as the "Prince of Ethics" and that the "Founding Father[s] [had an] explicit understanding of the duty of elected officials to publicly acknowledge God as the source of America's strength and direction."[62]

In the ultimate display authorized by the county officials after the first display had been struck down, the Ten Commandments were accompanied by framed copies of documents such as the Magna Carta and the Declaration of Independence, as well a statement saying, in part, "The Ten Commandments have profoundly influenced the formation of Western legal thought."[63] The posted version of the Ten Commandments was explicitly identified as the "King James Version" from the Book of Exodus.[64] The actual display was the following oddly edited excerpt of the verses in Exodus:

Thou shalt have no other gods before me.

Thou shalt not make unto thee any graven image, or any likeness of any thing that is in heaven above, or that is in the earth beneath, or that is in the water underneath the earth: Thou shalt not bow down thyself to them, nor serve them: for I the LORD thy God am a jealous God, visiting the iniquity of the fathers upon the children unto the third and fourth generation of them that hate me.

Thou shalt not take the name of the LORD thy God in vain: for the LORD will not hold him guiltless that taketh his name in vain.

Remember the Sabbath day, to keep it holy.

Honour thy father and thy mother: that thy days may be long upon the land which the LORD thy God giveth thee.

Thou shalt not kill.

Thou shalt not commit adultery.

Thou shalt not steal.

Thou shalt not bear false witness against thy neighbour.

Thou shalt not covet thy neighbour's house, thou shalt not covet th[y] neighbor's wife, nor his manservant, nor his maidservant, nor his ox, nor his ass, nor anything that is th[y] neighbour's.[65]

As with the Texas display, one notes immediately the striking omission of the explicit mandate that thou shalt not work on the Sabbath. As we will see, this inconvenient portion of the Ten Commandments has suffered greatly in contemporary legislation.

But surely the most striking aspect of the edited version chosen by Kentucky is the inclusion of the passage stating that God is a jealous God who visits iniquity unto four generations. Do those residents of Kentucky who view Jesus Christ as the Prince of Ethics really believe this? If so, why did they leave out the phrase that follows: "shewing mercy unto thousands [of generations] of them that love me, and keep my commandments"? It is hard to avoid the impression that many supporters of this display simply never read it.[66] In any event, this final Kentucky display of the Ten Commandments was struck down by the lower federal courts. It then ended up in the Supreme Court along with the Texas case.

From the point of view of clarity and guidance, the Supreme Court decisions in the Texas and Kentucky cases were failures. The Texas display was upheld, and the Kentucky display was struck down. Each decision was 5–4. In the Texas case, the justices wrote seven separate opinions; in the Kentucky case, they wrote three more. Thus, even justices who agreed with each other on the results often disagreed on the proper reasoning. Needless to say, litigation continues in the lower courts over Ten Commandments displays in a variety of settings.[67]

A semester or two of studying constitutional law might suffice for working through all of the arguments and precedents provided by the justices in the 2005 Ten Commandments cases. Fortunately, for our purposes, it will be enough to look at the broad themes presented in support of and opposition to the displays. This will give us a realistic sense of what will be won and what will be lost if the movement to post the Ten Commandments remains a priority for people of faith.

THE FOUR JUSTICES WHO
OPPOSED BOTH DISPLAYS

Let us begin with the major arguments put forth by the four justices— Stevens, O'Connor, Souter, and Ginsburg—who would have struck down both displays.[68] One of their points was the key argument in *Stone v. Graham*, the 1980 case that struck down the classroom display of the Ten Commandments. As with the majority in *Stone*, these four justices saw a purely religious purpose in the governmental decisions to post the commandments. The presence of other materials nearby, such as the Magna Carta, did not change the religious purpose, since the commandments, although they concern secular matters, obviously contain entirely religious dictates, such as the ban on graven images. In this view, some Ten Commandments displays, if they are merely symbolic representations of Moses carrying stone tablets alongside images of various secular lawgivers, might be acceptable.[69] But the Kentucky and Texas displays had no secular purpose.

The approach taken by these four justices includes the belief that the non–Establishment Clause prevents the government from preferring religion over nonreligion. In other words, there is an emphasis on government neutrality toward matters of faith and on the maintenance of a wall between church and state. Thus, the Texas monument is unacceptable because it stands on the grounds of the State Capitol and states in bold letters, "I AM the LORD thy God," before listing a variety of religious mandates.

Finally, Justice O'Connor, who was one of the four who opposed both displays, emphasized what has come to be known as the endorsement test. This approach has been adopted by several justices, so it remains quite important even though O'Connor is no longer on the Court. The endorsement test asks whether a reasonable observer, seeing the display, would believe that the government is "endorsing religion or a religious practice," thus "making adherence to religion relevant to a person's standing in the political community."[70]

This is the kind of legal test that turns very much on the specific facts of the case. In other settings, Justice O'Connor has upheld some religious displays but struck down others, depending on precisely what is in the entire display.[71] In particular, O'Connor has found in some cases that a combination of religious and nonreligious elements makes a display acceptable.[72] Here, however, O'Connor believed that a reasonable observer of the Ten Commandments displays in both the Kentucky courthouses and on the Texas State Capitol grounds would believe that the state governments in question were endorsing religion.[73]

THE FOUR JUSTICES ON THE OTHER SIDE

The four justices who would have allowed both displays—Rehnquist, Scalia, Kennedy, and Thomas—disagreed with their colleagues on the other side, in part, on factual questions.[74] In other words, to some extent they felt that the legislatures in question did not have a solely religious purpose or were not endorsing religion. But they disagreed more fundamentally as well.

As noted in *Stone v. Graham*, some justices would cease inquiring into legislative purpose in this setting. In addition, the justices who supported the Kentucky and Texas legislators believed that the displays should be judged in light of our nation's history.[75] Our leaders have, from the beginning, invoked God's name in connection with our nation. There was never a strict wall between church and state, nor should there be one now. These justices emphasized the large number of old Ten Commandments images one can find on government property around the country. Chief Justice Rehnquist noted, "We need only look within our own Courtroom. Since 1935, Moses has stood, holding two tablets that reveal portions of the Ten Commandments written in Hebrew, among other lawgivers in the south frieze."[76] Rehnquist went on to argue, "Of course, the Ten Commandments are religious. . . . But Moses was a lawgiver as well as a religious leader."[77]

For some supporters of this view, the non–Establishment Clause may bar government favoritism toward particular religious groups, but it does not prevent the government from statements or displays favoring religion over nonreligion. Justice Scalia, for example, emphasized that

"there is nothing unconstitutional in a State's favoring religion generally, honoring God through public prayer and acknowledgment, or, in a
non-proselytizing manner, venerating the Ten Commandments."[78] Scalia
relied, in part, on a strong tradition of presidential and congressional
statements that "have invoked God, but not Jesus Christ."[79]

Another important approach favored by some of these justices is to
say that the government violates the non–Establishment Clause only if
it coerces a religious practice or support for religion.[80] Thus, the government cannot make you pay taxes to provide the salaries for ministers,
nor can it make you engage in a prayer you disagree with. But passive
displays, such as the Ten Commandments, are not coercive. This coercion
test, which is closely associated with Justice Kennedy, but supported by
others as well, stands in sharp contrast to the endorsement test. Under
Kennedy's view, even if a reasonable observer believes that a Ten Commandments monument "endorses" religion over nonreligion, that is not
a reason to disallow the display, since the observer can simply avert his
or her eyes.[81] The observer is not being coerced to do anything.

Thus Kennedy, unlike O'Connor, has voted to uphold displays on
public property without engaging in a case-by-case analysis of whether the
symbols involved are overtly religious. Kennedy, however, does believe that
in some cases religious displays are impermissible because they amount
to proselytizing. As he wrote in one case, "[T]he [non–Establishment]
Clause forbids a city to permit the permanent erection of a large Latin
cross on the roof of city hall . . . because such an obtrusive year-round
religious display would place the government's weight behind an obvious effort to proselytize on behalf of a particular religion."[82]

JUSTICE BREYER IN THE MIDDLE

Finally, let us look at the views of Justice Breyer, the only member of the
Court who would have upheld one Ten Commandments display while
disallowing the other. Breyer joined Justice Souter's opinion for the Court
striking down the display in the Kentucky courthouses primarily on the
ground that this display had no secular purpose, that is, it was under-

taken solely for religious reasons.[83] But Breyer concurred in the decision to allow the Texas monument to stand. He said he found the Texas case "a borderline case," and he admitted that "in such cases, I see no test-related substitute for the exercise of legal judgment. . . . While the Court's prior tests provide useful guideposts—and might well lead to the same result the Court reaches today . . . —no exact formula can dictate a resolution to such fact-intensive cases."[84]

Justice Breyer then identified a number of facts that led him to uphold the Texas monument. He noted, for example, that in 1961 the state intended that the nonreligious aspects of the tablets' message predominate, that the tablets acknowledge that they were a gift of a private group, that the tablets were displayed in the midst of many other monuments that conveyed nonreligious themes, and that for forty years the monument had stood without protest.[85]

The last factor was the most important to Breyer. He noted that the display had stood "apparently uncontested for nearly two generations," and that "helps us understand that as a practical matter of *degree* this display is unlikely to prove divisive."[86] Breyer feared that ruling against the Texas display would exhibit "hostility to religion" and lead to the sort of divisiveness the Establishment Clause seeks to avoid, because if the Texas display had to come down, that "might well encourage disputes concerning the removal of longstanding depictions of the Ten Commandments from public buildings across the Nation."[87]

THE FUTURE OF TEN COMMANDMENTS DISPLAYS

It is easy to make light of the Supreme Court's divided and imprecise reaction to the Ten Commandments cases it confronted in 1980 and 2005. But I would be hard pressed to come up with a legal theory that would satisfy any nine strong-minded individuals in this difficult area. It is simply not possible to predict how the Court will rule the next time it considers a Ten Commandments case. There have been changes in the Court's membership since the Texas and Kentucky cases. Moreover, the justices who remain on the Court have virtually all committed themselves to approaches that will turn on the specific facts of the display before them. Not only Justice Breyer looks closely at the precise setting and history of the case. Justice Souter, who voted against both displays, emphasized that some displays, such as those that presented the Ten Commandments symbolically as part of a set of images including secular lawmakers, would be acceptable. Justice Kennedy, who voted for both, has said that permanent displays could be unacceptable when they amounted to proselytizing.

Some religious groups may have chosen to support posting the Ten Commandments because it is a relatively ecumenical document: it plays an important role in both Judaism and Christianity, and it overlaps with the teachings of many other faiths. As a matter of litigation strategy, this made sense. Justice Scalia, who supports the constitutionality of the displays, said that they amount to a public recognition of God. He emphasized that our traditions do not look as favorably on government recognition of Jesus.[88]

But this ecumenical consensus is purchased at a cost. If your display actually contains the text of the Ten Commandments, you run into real difficulties because of the different versions of the text in the Bible, the difficulties posed by translation, and, most important, the difficult and controversial teachings contained in the commandments. This explains why some Christian and Jewish groups have opposed Ten Commandments displays.[89] And when you turn to other religions, it is just not possible to maintain with a straight face that the Ten Commandments is composed of teachings that everyone shares. Not every faith bans bowing to graven images; indeed, not every faith accepts the Lord who announces, "I am the LORD thy God, which have brought thee out of the land of Egypt." This specific religious narrative is not how everyone sees the history of humankind.

To get a sense of the specific context of the biblical narrative, re-read the commandment on honoring your parents: "Honour thy father and thy mother: that thy days may be long upon the land which the LORD thy God giveth thee." According to some commentators, "the land which the LORD thy God giveth thee" refers to God giving Israel to the Jewish people, a belief that is not shared by all Jews, let alone by everyone else.[90]

Nonetheless, it is certainly possible that some future Ten Commandments displays on public property will be upheld in the Supreme Court. Displays like the one in Texas that have been around for decades without arousing protest are most likely to survive; however, it may also be possible to successfully create a new display. Indeed, it is possible to see the factors that will characterize such displays.

If you want a display upheld, use as little of the text of the commandments as possible. Emulate those old displays on courthouses that just show two tablets with the numbers 1 through 10, or perhaps a Hebrew letter standing for each commandment. Surround the image of the tablets with pictures of other important laws, such as the Magna Carta, the Constitution, or modern civil rights laws. If Moses appears, make sure you also have Hammurabi, James Madison, or Lyndon Johnson. After the Supreme Court decisions in 2005, the Louisiana legislature authorized posting a version of the commandments in public buildings along with the Declaration of Independence, the Mayflower Compact, and the Northwest Ordinance.[91]

This game is not worth the prize. I know that symbols are important and that for many people of faith, the desire to post the Ten Commandments is a desire to make a symbolic statement about the role of God in modern life. But symbols can swamp reality. There are limitless opportunities in private homes and places of worship to post and study the real Ten Commandments. Posting a hollow imitation in the public square is a victory for secularism, not for religion. Reducing the Ten Commandments to the vague symbolism of the Nike Swoosh is not a worthy goal.

OBEYING THE TEN COMMANDMENTS
IN MODERN AMERICA

It might seem too obvious for words that Americans are free to obey the Ten Commandments, and in most cases it is. The government does not force you, for example, to take the Lord's name in vain or to believe in many gods. The government even reinforces some biblical commandments, such as the ban on theft, with its own criminal code because there are secular as well as religious reasons to oppose theft.

But what about those relatively rare cases where the government's relationship to one of the Ten Commandments is more controversial? Here, American history teaches a surprising lesson. Despite the rhetoric so popular today, we cannot blame the unelected courts for our problems. More often than not, the political officials we elect have undermined observance. In Pogo's immortal words, "We have met the enemy and he is us."

Consider the efforts by Jehovah's Witnesses to obey the commandment that forbids bowing down to graven images.[92] The Witnesses, a Christian group, believe the Bible is the supreme authority, and they interpret this commandment as forbidding them to salute the American flag. They further believe that the free exercise of religion and the freedom of speech and association guaranteed them by the Constitution allow them to live by their interpretation of this commandment. After all, it is not as if their religion is teaching them to harm others. In that kind of situation we would all agree the state can step in. But here, the Witnesses just seek to be excused from the flag salute that starts the day in public school.

When, prior to World War II, the Witnesses began to have problems with the government over this issue, the text of the Pledge of Allegiance was virtually the same as it is today. The only real difference was that the pledge did not contain "under God."[93] That phrase, which was added in 1954, does not matter one way or another to the Witnesses. Whether or not we describe the nation as "under God," we are pledging "allegiance to the flag," and the Witnesses believe the Ten Commandments forbid them from doing that.

You might hope that local officials, aware of the virtues of religious faith, would craft exemptions to the pledge requirement. But in 1937, Jehovah's Witnesses Lillian Gobitis, age twelve, and her brother William, age ten, were expelled from the public schools of Minersville, Pennsylvania, for refusing to salute the flag as required by local law. They challenged this decision in court, and in 1940, the Supreme Court ruled against them.[94] Justice Frankfurter wrote the opinion for the Court. Only Justice Stone dissented. Frankfurter argued that religious belief could not routinely excuse you from the demands of the state, citing the Court's nineteenth-century affirmation of antipolygamy laws. Frankfurter believed that the legislature had the right to require the pledge in the interest of building national unity. Finally, Frankfurter made an argument for leaving the matter to the elected branches of government:

[T]o the legislature no less than to courts is committed the guardianship of deeply-cherished liberties. . . . When all the effective means of inducing political changes are left free from interference, education in the abandonment of foolish legislation is itself a training in liberty. To fight out the wise use of legislative authority in the forum of public opinion and before legislative assemblies rather than to transfer such a contest to the judicial arena, serves to vindicate the self-confidence of a free people.[95]

Apparently Frankfurter believed that the legislatures would see the wisdom of allowing students to be excused from the pledge, a power the legislatures undoubtedly had. But something very different happened. In fact, something very frightening happened.

More states, not fewer, adopted mandatory flag-salute laws.[96] The laws were even toughened. Whereas the Gobitis children were expelled from public school and thus forced to go to private school, some new laws threatened children with reformatories and parents with punishment for causing delinquency if the flag was not saluted. There was an outbreak of violence against Jehovah's Witnesses. One of their meeting halls was burned to the ground in Maine, Witnesses were beaten and castrated by vigilantes in Nebraska, and at times, the police aided the mobs rather than the Witnesses.

This extraordinary outburst was fueled by a surge of patriotism in the years leading up to World War II. It is remarkable how little we learned from the events in Europe. Germany banned the Jehovah's Witnesses in 1933, in part for refusing to give the Nazi salute. Thousands of Witnesses were later sent to concentration camps. And it is worth noting that our flag salute in those days was similar to the Nazi salute: when you pledged the flag in an American school, you used a "stiff-arm salute" with the right hand raised and the palm turned up.

Now I realize that the Jehovah's Witnesses are a minority religion, and one that is not popular with some other Christians, as well as with some non-Christians. Moreover, I realize that their reading of the commandment that forbids bowing down to graven images is not the most common reading. But the Witnesses' practice does involve the Ten Commandments, and the reaction of American legislatures in the 1940s to that practice makes me wonder how many Americans are serious about respecting the Ten Commandments as opposed to posting them. Perhaps American citizens give more respect to the actual Ten Commandments today than they did sixty years ago. Perhaps.

In any event, the Supreme Court bailed us out of this dark chapter in American history.[97] In 1942, the West Virginia legislature ordered that the flag salute be made mandatory in public schools. The statute provided that failure to conform was "insubordination" dealt with by expulsion. In the meantime, the expelled child was "unlawfully absent" and could be prosecuted as a delinquent. The parents were also liable for prosecution and for a jail term if convicted.

A challenge to the West Virginia law was brought and reached the Supreme Court in 1943. Three justices in the *Gobitis* majority had retired, and two others changed their minds. The Court, in an extraordinarily rare event, overruled the *Gobitis* decision even though it was only three years old. Over the dissent of three justices (including Justice Frankfurter), Justice Jackson's opinion for the Court held that students had a constitutional right to be excused from the pledge, a right that remains in place to this day. Jackson did not focus on religious freedom exclusively, holding more broadly that the pledge improperly compelled people to express sentiments with which they disagreed:

If there is any fixed star in our constitutional constellation, it is that no official, high or petty, can prescribe what shall be orthodox in politics, nationalism, religion, or other matters of opinion or force citizens to confess by word or act their faith therein. If there are any circumstances which permit an exception, they do not now occur to us.

We think the action of the local authorities in compelling the flag salute and pledge transcends constitutional limitations on their power and invades the sphere of intellect and spirit which it is the purpose of the First Amendment to our Constitution to reserve from all official control.[98]

THE DEMISE OF SABBATH OBSERVANCE

The graven images dispute does not stand alone. In a far broader confrontation between the Ten Commandments and American law, once again the unelected Court supported religious practice, and the elected legislatures made that practice more difficult. The issue here is Sabbath observance, where we see today a continuing erosion of religious practice. The Ten Commandments spend more time on Sabbath observance than any other matter. In Exodus we are told not only to remember the Sabbath day and instructed in detail to avoid work but we are also given the rationale that the Lord himself rested on that day. In Deuteronomy we are told to keep the Sabbath, and we are given another rationale: the Sabbath is designed to commemorate the Lord leading the people of Israel out of Egypt.

Now few Christians (and few Jews) follow the Orthodox Jewish practice of strictly avoiding all work and commerce on the Sabbath, even to the point of not turning on a light switch or answering a telephone. But for centuries Christians of all backgrounds took Sabbath observance quite seriously. Christianity early on moved the day of rest to Sunday.[99] It became not only a day to go to church but a day to stay home with the family. From colonial times to the second half of the twentieth century, the secular government supported Sabbath observance.[100]

This governmental support for Christian observance of the Lord's day was not subtle. Pennsylvania law, for example, provided fines and imprisonment for "whoever does or performs any worldly employment or business whatsoever on the Lord's day, commonly called Sunday (works of necessity and charity only excepted), or uses or practices any game, hunting, shooting, sport or diversion whatsoever on the same day not authorized by law."[101] Laws like this one were called Sunday Closing Laws or Sunday Blue Laws. They included various exceptions and differed somewhat from state to state. Nonetheless, in the middle of the twentieth century, the majority of the states had laws that broadly banned working, employing others, or being open for business on Sunday.[102]

In 1961, the Supreme Court considered a set of cases challenging the Sunday Closing Laws in Pennsylvania, Maryland, and Massachusetts on constitutional grounds.[103] These challenges called into question every Sunday Blue Law in the nation. The central argument of the opponents of the Blue Laws was that the laws violated the separation of church and state. The laws were said to be an establishment of religion because they put the state's power, indeed its criminal laws, behind the religious practice of observing the Sabbath as commanded by the Ten Commandments. And some of the challengers were Orthodox Jewish businesspeople who also raised a free exercise of religion argument. Because their religious practice required them to be closed on Saturday, they suffered an important competitive disadvantage when the government forced them to close on Sunday as well: they could be open only five days a week, whereas other stores could be open six.

The chief justice of the Supreme Court when these cases were decided was Earl Warren. One year later, the Warren Court decided that prayer in the public schools, a practice in the United States that went back to colonial times, was an unconstitutional establishment of religion even though students could be excused from the prayers. For better or for worse, Earl Warren is widely viewed as strongly favoring the separation of church and state. So what did the Warren Court do about the Sunday Closing Laws? They upheld every one of them. In a series of four decisions handed down on the same day, they rejected every challenge to those laws.[104] Earl Warren himself wrote the lead opinion in every case. There were dissents, but in this area of the law, the Court was clear: Sunday Blue Laws were constitutional.

On the establishment of religion claim, Warren admitted that the Blue Laws were "undeniably religious in origin."[105] He could hardly claim otherwise. In Maryland, for example, the laws went back to colonial times, when the state had an established religion; the relevant statute was titled "An Act for the Service of Almighty God and the Establishment of the Protestant Religion within this Province" and went on to state the importance of keeping the Lord's day holy and sanctified.[106]

But this does not resolve the constitutional issue. As we have seen, laws against stealing might have a religious basis, but they do not constitute an establishment of religion because they serve secular purposes as well, such as the functioning of a vibrant economy. A law is suspect under the non–Establishment Clause when it has no secular purpose and is designed to serve solely religious aims. Earl Warren argued that Sunday Closing Laws had a secular purpose. He noted that labor unions supported these laws as an improvement for workers' lives, whether or not the workers are religious. Viewed as labor laws, Blue Laws are not fundamentally different from maximum hour laws generally.

Why not have the state simply mandate that everyone gets one day off a week without specifying the day? Warren argued that a state could believe that a day of rest works best when everybody rests on the same day. Should the state be required to choose a common day that has no religious significance? Warren replied that Sunday had become the day of rest for nonreligious and religious people alike, and he concluded that it would be "unrealistic for enforcement purposes and perhaps detrimental to the general welfare to require a State to choose a common day of rest other than that which most persons would select of their own accord."[107]

As to the free exercise of religion claim by the Orthodox Jewish businesspeople, Warren argued that the state had not interfered with their beliefs and that any burden on their religious practice was indirect. The state was not forcing them to work on Saturday, their Sabbath. It is inevitable, Warren argued, that in "a cosmopolitan nation made up of people of almost every conceivable religious preference" laws would "result in an economic disadvantage to some religious sects and not to others."[108] He gave the example of tax laws that limit the amount that may be deducted for religious contributions even though some faiths may require greater donations.[109]

Whether you agree with Earl Warren or not, the key to understanding his Supreme Court opinions upholding Sunday Closing Laws is the description he gave of the virtues of a day of rest:

[T]he state seeks to set one day apart from all others as a day of rest, repose, recreation and tranquility—a day which all members of the family and community have the opportunity to spend and enjoy together, a day on which there exists relative quiet and disassociation from the everyday intensity of commercial activities, a day on which people may visit friends and relatives who are not available during working days.[110]

So the Supreme Court, in 1961, greatly facilitated the ability of Americans to obey the Ten Commandments. In a majority Christian nation, the people were free to attend church and observe the Sabbath on Sunday without employers forcing them to work or stores luring them to shop. And what happened? The people repealed the Sunday Closing Laws. Of course, a few remain. You might have trouble in some parts of the country buying some kinds of alcohol on Sunday. But let us be honest: stores are crowded, people are at work, and Sunday is about as restful as Tuesday. Maybe less so.

There are any number of reasons why the Sunday Closing Laws were gradually repealed.[111] Two-career families find it harder to shop during the week. Shopping malls are increasingly located far from where people work. Or maybe people simply do not want to spend a quiet day with friends and relatives.

But the examples of those who would not bow to a graven image by saluting the flag and those who would not profane the Lord's Day by working on Sunday still convey a message. The Supreme Court may have made it difficult to post the Ten Commandments in public places, but do not blame the Court if those commandments are not followed. Americans have a constitutional right to practice our religion. But many of us would rather post the commandments in a public building than read them or obey them.

CHAPTER 3

How Intelligent Design Demeans Religion

THE MOVEMENT TO TEACH intelligent design in the public schools is often seen as a successor to the efforts to teach the Genesis account of creation in those schools. In both cases, the goal is to undermine the theory of evolution. There is a great deal of truth in this, and thus it is not surprising that forcing intelligent design into the public school science curriculum has run into trouble in the courts.

But the reality is much worse. The Book of Genesis is an extraordinarily influential religious text that remains of great importance to countless people of faith. It will survive its absence from ninth-grade biology class. Intelligent design, on the other hand, empties religion of everything that makes it important. God is no longer the creator of the universe, a source of ethical teachings, or the inspiration for a sense of awe and humility. God is instead a second-rate engineer who created the bacterial flagellum, a tiny propeller attached to the rear of some bacteria.

The modern intelligent design movement claims to show gaps in the Darwinian account of evolution, and its supporters therefore demand that it be taught as a corrective to evolution in the public schools. We will begin by looking at the intelligent design movement in the context of earlier attacks on Darwin and the fate of those attacks in the courts. We will then see why intelligent design has had problems in litigation, but more important, we will see why it is so destructive of actual religious faith.

Next we will try to understand the remarkable durability of the disputes over Darwin's work by looking at evolution's ties to the question of human origins and to the unhappy history of social Darwinism and eugenics. Neither of these connections justifies the intelligent design movement, but they are worthy of attention in their own right. Indeed, we will see that scientists have a special interest in the topic of human origins that is similar to the interest of Darwin's opponents.

We will then turn to the original argument from design, a much more serious and enduring notion than so-called intelligent design. We will see that the argument from design is a religious argument that continues to inspire millions. And we will see that many modern scientists, from Einstein to superstring theorists, profess a sense of faith and wonder in the order of the universe that is notably absent from the disfigured teachings that result when religion is forced into the public school curriculum. The faith of scientists does not belong in a public school biology class any more than Genesis does, but it is beautifully expressed in other settings, a lesson from which many religious leaders could learn.

THE PATH FROM GENESIS TO THE COURTROOM

There is much support for the widely held view that intelligent design is just the latest effort to force the Bible into the public schools as a counterweight to Darwin. So let us begin with that part of the story.

Darwin's publication of *On the Origin of Species* in 1859 caused immediate controversy.[1] The idea that all life, including human life, developed through millions of years of natural selection upset many settled beliefs. Darwin's argument for what he called "descent with modification" turned on the belief that those organisms with characteristics that gave them an advantage in staying alive in a particular environment were more likely to pass on their traits to their descendants. Mutations that arose randomly could create such characteristics. Largely through this process, life on earth evolved. Today, greatly strengthened by the discovery of the genetic basis of inheritance and by much testing, the theory of evolution is fundamental to understanding modern biology.[2]

Evolution contradicts the biblical account of the creation of life if that account is taken literally. The Bible assumes creation in six days, with a special creation for humans.[3] Moreover, the Bible is read by some to teach that the earth is only about six thousand years old.[4] Of course, many ideas in modern science are inconsistent with a literal reading of the Bible. Scientists do not believe, for example, that the sun stood still so that Joshua could win a battle.[5] But opposition to the theory of evolution is obviously deeper and more important to millions of people. They believe that kinship between humans and primates diminishes humankind. We are not, they argue, just advanced apes, with no special status or fate.

From the beginning to the present day, many—perhaps most—Christians and Jews have reconciled evolution with their belief in God. Evolution could simply be God's method of creation. If humans have characteristics that other creatures lack—such as a soul—God could have endowed humans with those characteristics outside the operation of evolution. The theory of evolution need not contradict these beliefs. Indeed, as a scientific theory, it does not speak to matters of faith. In particular, it does not speak to metaphysical beliefs, such as the existence of the soul, which cannot be tested. For this reason, the Catholic Church, as well as countless Protestant and Jewish believers, has not opposed the scientific account of the evolution of the species.[6] Indeed, in recent years, prominent scientists have written heartfelt books explaining that they are believing Christians who believe as well in evolution.[7]

But to millions of others, evolution is offensive, and therefore it must be wrong. This deeply held belief helped fuel the development in nineteenth-century America of fundamentalism, a type of evangelical Protestantism that stresses a literal interpretation of the Bible.[8] In the 1920s, a surge in fundamentalism inspired legislators to strike out at Darwinism. In 1925, Tennessee adopted a law that made it a misdemeanor punishable by fine to teach in the public schools of that state "any theory that denies the story of the divine creation of man as taught in the Bible and to teach instead that man has descended from a lower order of animals."[9]

When John Thomas Scopes went on trial for violating this law, the ensuing "monkey trial" gripped the nation.[10] William Jennings Bryan appeared on behalf of the Tennessee law, and the famed criminal defense attorney Clarence Darrow defended Scopes.[11] The jury convicted Scopes, but the Tennessee Supreme Court in 1927, while not questioning the underlying law, set aside the conviction on the ground that the judge rather than the jury had imposed the one hundred–dollar fine in violation of Tennessee law.[12] The Tennessee court then noted that Scopes no longer worked for the state and concluded, "We see nothing to be gained by prolonging the life of this bizarre case. On the contrary, we think the peace and dignity of the state, which all criminal prosecutions are brought to redress, will be better conserved [if charges are dropped]."[13]

The case against Scopes ended there, but the controversy did not. Other anti-evolution laws remained on the books. In 1965, Susan Epperson, a tenth-grade biology teacher in Little Rock, Arkansas, planned to teach evolution to her students, but she was concerned about a 1929 Arkansas statute that made it unlawful for any public school teacher "to teach the theory or doctrine that mankind ascended or descended from a lower order of animals."[14] Epperson brought a lawsuit that ended up in the United States Supreme Court.[15]

The Court, in a 1968 opinion by Justice Fortas, found that the Arkansas law violated the United States Constitution's ban on established religion.[16] Although the law did not explicitly mention the Bible, the Court was convinced that the law was motivated by support for the Genesis account of creation:

[T]he First Amendment does not permit the State to require that teaching and learning must be tailored to the principles or prohibitions of any sect or dogma. . . . [T]here can be no doubt that Arkansas has sought to prevent its teachers from discussing the theory of evolution because it is contrary to the belief of some that the Book of Genesis must be the exclusive source of doctrine as to the origin of man. No suggestion has been made that Arkansas' law may be justified by considerations of state policy other than the religious views of some of its citizens.[17]

Justice Fortas suggested that perhaps the Arkansas statute was "presently more of a curiosity than a vital fact of life."[18] Just like the Tennessee judges, he obviously hoped that the "peace and dignity" of our society could be spared further disputes over monkeys and humans. But also like the Tennessee judges, his hope that this matter would just go away was not to be fulfilled.

Indeed, only a few years later the Tennessee legislature reacted to Fortas's opinion. That opinion had effectively voided the 1925 Tennessee statute used to prosecute John Thomas Scopes. So in 1973, Tennessee enacted a new law that allowed evolution in the classroom, but only if the teacher also gave preferential treatment to the Genesis account of creation.[19]

This elaborate statute worked as follows. First, the law said that any biology textbook used in the public schools that expressed "a theory about origins or creation of man" had to contain a specific disclaimer stating that this "is a theory . . . and is not represented to be scientific fact."[20] The same textbook also had to give "an equal amount of emphasis on the origins and creation of man and his world as the same is recorded in other theories, including, but not limited to, the Genesis account in the Bible."[21] The statute specifically said that the biblical account "shall not be required to carry the disclaimer" about just being a "theory" and not "scientific fact."[22] Finally, the statute said that the "teaching of all occult or satanical beliefs of human origin is expressly excluded from this Act."[23]

Unsurprisingly, this statute was quickly struck down in court. When, in 1975, the federal court of appeals heard a challenge to the law, the court began by stating that "the purpose of establishing the Biblical version of the creation of man over the Darwinian theory of the evolution of man is as clear in the 1973 statute as it was in the statute of 1925."[24] The court noted that the statute was designed to cast the Genesis account in a more favorable light than evolution by requiring a disclaimer only for the latter.[25] Moreover, the court was deeply troubled by the exclusion of "occult or satanical beliefs":

Throughout human history the God of some men has frequently been regarded as the Devil incarnate by men of other religious persuasions. It would be utterly impossible for the Tennessee Textbook Commission to determine which religious theories were "occult" or "satanical" without seeking to resolve the theological arguments which have embroiled and frustrated theologians through the ages.[26]

The court had put its finger on a real problem. The Book of Genesis is hardly the only account of the origin of humans that differs from Darwin's. There are ancient creation narratives in the Hindu and Native American traditions, for example, that differ from those of both Darwin and the Bible.[27] The legislators in Tennessee were being sincere when they presented the Bible as the only account that had to be taught and that would not be coupled with a disclaimer, but they were creating a form of public education that is not consistent with America's diversity or its constitutional system.

CREATION SCIENCE ENTERS THE PICTURE

Thus, by 1975, it was pretty clear that state legislatures could not keep Darwin out of the public schools in order to further the view of creation that follows from a literal reading of Genesis. Fundamentalist opponents of evolution then turned to the remarkable movement called creation science.[28] The publication in 1961 of *The Genesis Flood* by John C. Whitcomb Jr. and Henry M. Morris marks the beginning of "scientific creationism."[29] The themes of the book are familiar. The authors believe that the earth is only a few thousand years old and that there were literally six days of creation, each exactly twenty-four hours long, just as spelled out in Genesis.[30] Not all religious opponents of Darwin take the Bible literally in this sense, but Whitcomb and Flood were hardly alone in their view of the matter.

What made *The Genesis Flood* remarkable was that the authors presented their case as a series of scientific arguments in favor of their beliefs. Morris, a Ph.D. engineer, and Whitcomb, a theologian, believed that conventional science demonstrated the literal truth of Genesis.[31] They argued, for example, that Noah's Flood created the fossil record, that ancient land bridges explain how kangaroos made it into the Ark, that the Ark itself had a displacement tonnage (using the Hebrew rather than the Babylonian cubit) of 19,940 tons, that the Van Allen radiation belt undermines radioactive dating mechanisms, and so on.[32]

The arguments in *The Genesis Flood* persuaded virtually no one in the traditional scientific community.[33] Countless opponents of Darwin are also unpersuaded, as we will see when we look at the very different beliefs of the intelligent design movement. Not only is the evidence in *The Genesis Flood* unconvincing but the authors' approach undermines their scientific stance. They begin the book, after all, by saying that they write "from the perspective of full belief in the complete divine inspiration and perspicuity of Scripture. . . . Our conclusions must unavoidably be colored by our Biblical presuppositions, and this we plainly acknowledge."[34]

But *The Genesis Flood* is not only bad science. It is a remarkable capitulation by religion to the scientific worldview. For many who believe literally in the Bible, science is beside the point. Faith is what matters. God may operate in ways we cannot understand; all of our much-touted science may mislead us. These people of faith would never concede that some new discovery about ancient floods could falsify the Book of Genesis, but that is the logical consequence of the approach taken in *The Genesis Flood*. No wonder there are devout Christians who bluntly reject the Morris and Whitcomb approach, arguing that it is "impious and just plain stupid to try to prove from science that the Word of God is true."[35] Nonetheless, in an amazing testimony to the American belief that everything is improved by calling it science, the kind of work exemplified by *The Genesis Flood* became popular with some fundamentalists beginning in the 1960s. Groups like the Institute for Creation Research and the Creation Research Society began to argue for the study of the scientific basis of Genesis.[36]

This approach was seized on by legislatures who, despite their recent reversals in court, wanted to have public schools undermine Darwin for religious reasons. Thus, in 1981, Arkansas, which had lost the 1968 *Epperson* case in the United States Supreme Court, enacted the Balanced Treatment for Creation-Science and Evolution-Science Act.[37] This act, which was based on a model statute considered by several legislatures, defined "creation-science" as "the scientific evidence for creation [that] includes . . . the insufficiency of mutation and natural selection in bringing about development of all living things. . . . Separate ancestry for man and apes. . . . Explanation of the earth's geology by catastrophism, including the occurrence of a worldwide flood . . . a relatively recent inception of the earth."[38] Under the act, no public school could teach evolution unless it also gave equal time to creation science.[39]

Many supporters of this statute clearly had no real use for the kind of analysis that Morris and Whitcomb championed. The primary draftsman of the model statute on which the Arkansas law was based wrote, "While neither evolution nor creation can qualify as a scientific theory . . . we have freely used these terms—the evolution theory and the theory of scientific creationism—in the bill's text," and "we're not making any scientific claims for creation, but we are challenging evolution's claim to be scientific."[40] Perhaps a few supporters of Arkansas's new law were interested in what the Van Allen radiation belt teaches about the age of the earth, but most were simply believers in the Bible who were looking for a legally acceptable way to shape the public school curriculum. Dressing up Genesis as science might be demeaning, but perhaps it would work in court.

It did not. By 1982, the act had been struck down by a federal district court. The judge canvassed the history of the Arkansas law and had no difficulty finding that it was intended to promote the fundamentalist religious belief in Genesis.[41] He noted that although a scientific theory like evolution is "tentative and always subject to revision or abandonment in light of facts that are inconsistent with, or falsify, the theory . . . [t]he "creationists' methods do not take data, weigh it against the opposing scientific data, and thereafter reach the conclusion stated. . . . Instead, they take the literal wording of the Book of Genesis and attempt to find scientific support for it."[42]

As a factual matter, it is hard to quarrel with the judges' view. The proponents of the Arkansas law would have been horrified at the suggestion that Genesis could be proven wrong in a laboratory. They called their beliefs "scientific" only in order to get them into public school. Moreover, they did not call for equal study of all creation narratives, only the one that includes Noah's Flood and a young earth.

At about the same time that the Arkansas law was being struck down in district court, the Louisiana legislature was enacting its own Balanced Treatment for Creation-Science and Evolution-Science in Public School Instruction law.[43] Because it was based on the same model act being promoted by various religious groups, the Louisiana law was virtually identical to the Arkansas enactment. Litigation over the Louisiana law reached the United States Supreme Court, which struck it down in 1987.[44]

The Supreme Court's reasoning was similar to that employed by the judge in Arkansas. Justice Brennan's opinion for the Court noted that Louisiana had singled out only "creation-science" to "balance" evolution.[45] The Court, he said, "need not be blind . . . to the legislature's preeminent religious purpose in enacting this statute."[46] As with the earlier laws that banned the teaching of Darwin's theories, the Louisiana law "selects from the body of knowledge a particular segment which it proscribes for the sole reason that it is deemed to conflict with . . . a particular interpretation of the Book of Genesis by a particular religious group."[47] The Supreme Court noted that a public school could teach "scientific critiques of prevailing scientific theories."[48] But the Court believed that because the Louisiana Act was designed instead "to endorse a particular religious doctrine, the Act furthers religion in violation of the Establishment Clause."[49]

INTELLIGENT DESIGN AND THE
DOVER, PENNSYLVANIA, LITIGATION

By this time, judges were no longer saying that their latest decision would end the controversy over Darwin. Everyone was starting to understand that feelings ran too deep on this issue. Not long after creation science met a roadblock in the courts, efforts began to teach intelligent design in the public schools instead. When the Dover, Pennsylvania, school board ordered in 2004 that intelligent design be taught in the public schools, a lawsuit quickly followed. When a federal judge then struck down the school board's order, he relied on the numerous precedents we have seen concerning religious attacks on evolution. Under the circumstances, his decision was not surprising.

The authorities in the Dover Area public school system had passed a resolution stating, "Students will be made aware of gaps/problems in Darwin's theory and of other theories of evolution including, but not limited to, intelligent design." The school board also required that ninth-grade biology teachers read a statement to their students that included this assertion: "Intelligent Design is an explanation of the origin of life that differs from Darwin's view. The reference book, *Of Pandas and People*, is available for students who might be interested in gaining an understanding of what Intelligent Design actually involves."[50]

The modern idea of "intelligent design" came into use after the Supreme Court's 1987 decision voiding Louisiana's effort to teach creation science in the public schools.[51] Supporters of intelligent design argue that natural selection cannot explain the existence of certain complex features in some biological organisms.[52] They argue further that the existence of these features shows that they were designed by an intelligent agent, not by the process of evolution.[53] These supporters often refer to this agent as God, but in some settings, and in the book *Of Pandas and People*, the word *God* is avoided.[54]

The leading example of the kind of feature stressed by the intelligent design movement is the flagella of bacteria, which are like outboard motors that bacterial cells use to propel themselves.[55] For this system to work, many parts—such as the molecular motor that causes rotation of the flagellum, and the proteins that hold the motor in place—must all work together.[56] Supporters of intelligent design maintain that this type of "irreducible complexity" could not have come about by evolution. How could all of the working parts have emerged at once? There must, it is contended, have been an intelligent designer.[57] Evolutionary biologists argue that complex systems of this type can emerge when a preexisting part that had one function takes on a new function.[58] For example, the mammalian middle-ear bones evolved from what had been jawbones.[59] In the case of the flagellum, a precursor may have functioned not as a rotary motor but as a secretory system.[60]

In its broadest outlines, intelligent design does not dispute that every organism on earth, including humans, might have evolved from earlier organisms or that this might have taken place over millions of years. But supporters of the theory want to teach public school students that only an "intelligent designer" can explain the gaps in current Darwinian accounts of certain features in living organisms.[61]

The judge in the Dover litigation was confronted not with an abstract theory but with the actual intelligent design policy and book mandated by the school board. He had little difficulty striking down the school board's actions. The judge emphasized that intelligent design (ID) had emerged just after the Supreme Court's 1987 decision striking down the teaching of creation science.[62] He found that the book endorsed by the school board, *Of Pandas and People*, went through several drafts, some completed before and some after that decision.[63] In comparing the pre- and post-decision drafts, he found that "three astonishing points emerge: (1) the definition for creation science in early drafts is identical to the definition of ID; (2) cognates of the word creation (creationism and creationist), which appeared approximately 150 times, were deliberately and systematically replaced with the phrase ID; and (3) the changes occurred shortly after the Supreme Court held that creation science is religion and cannot be taught in public school science classes."[64]

The court found that "the overwhelming evidence at trial established that ID is a religious view, a mere re-labeling of creationism, and not a scientific theory."[65] Leading scientific groups had rejected the notion that ID was a science. It was not testable, nor did it lead to peer-reviewed publications.[66] ID was based, the judge said, "upon a false dichotomy, namely that to the extent evolutionary theory is discredited, ID is confirmed."[67] The court had no difficulty in concluding that the board members who put ID in the Dover public schools were not interested in raising the level of scientific literacy in the student body. One had openly called "creationism" his

number-one issue, whereas another had said, "I challenge you . . . to trace
your roots to the monkey you came from. . . . 2,000 years ago someone
died on a cross. Can't someone take a stand for him?"[68] More broadly, the
court found that "the writings of leading ID proponents reveal that the
designer postulated by their argument is the God of Christianity."[69]

The judge concluded that the Dover policy had the purpose of advancing religion and that it endorsed religion in violation of the non–
Establishment Clause of the Constitution, as that clause had been
interpreted by the United States Supreme Court.[70] He ended his opinion
with a virtual shout of frustration:

> [L]eading proponents of ID make a bedrock assumption which is utterly false.
> Their presupposition is that evolutionary theory is antithetical to a belief in
> the existence of a supreme being and to religion in general. Repeatedly in this
> trial, Plaintiffs' scientific experts testified that the theory of evolution . . . in no
> way conflicts with, nor does it deny, the existence of a divine creator. . . . The
> students, parents, and teachers of the Dover Area School District deserved
> better than to be dragged into this legal maelstrom, with its resulting utter
> waste of monetary and personal resources.[71]

INTELLIGENT DESIGN VERSUS RELIGION

Just before the federal district judge's decision, the voters in Dover, Pennsylvania, replaced the school board with one that did not seek to teach
intelligent design.[72] Thus, there was no appeal, and intelligent design
was dormant in the public schools for a time. But it will not be dormant
for long. Its supporters remain determined to push their ideas. People of
faith should be very afraid of the possibility that intelligent design will
someday work its way into the public schools. It would be hard to imagine a more unattractive set of ideas. Intelligent design is a particularly
unappealing version of the old idea of a "God of the gaps," an idea with
little support among modern clergy or theologians.[73] If ancient people
could not explain thunder, they attributed it to the gods. When science
explained thunder, God became the explanation for eclipses, until science explained them. And so on.

With intelligent design God is introduced to explain gaps in Darwinian explanations of organisms. Of course, there are such gaps, and scientists are always working on filling them, either with existing theories or with new ones. Until they do, God is the explanation for the bacterium's flagellum. But he's not called God. He is an "intelligent designer." In theory, he could be an alien, and he designs only those odd things evolution cannot explain. He gets no credit for human arms or legs. And he is not a very good designer. He creates people with unexplained genetic diseases, as well as entire species that die out.[74] Moreover, it is not even clear that he works alone. Intelligent design fits with the idea of two or more designers, and it leaves open the possibility that the designer was himself created by another designer.

No one believes this. It does not represent the real religious faith that nourishes millions of Americans. That faith exists outside science, because it does not speak to questions that science can answer and it does not turn on the results of laboratory experiments. Science can neither prove nor disprove the existence of God, the divinity of Christ, the nature of the soul, or any of the other teachings of actual religions. Science cannot provide the sense of humility or the guidance on how to live our lives that these religions provide.

The second-rate engineer with no name—the God in a witness protection program—conjured up by intelligent design is the ludicrous cost of forcing religion into the public sphere. It is not worth it. Intelligent design is religion as a litigation strategy. It tries to unite religious opponents of Darwin by papering over disagreements about the age of the earth and whether evolution took place at all. Even at this level, intelligent design is not able to hold together. Consider the words of Henry M. Morris, coauthor of *The Genesis Flood*, believer in the biblical account of creation and the leading proponent of creation science:

ID people . . . feel it best to leave the Bible and Biblical God out of the argument entirely. Some even feel that evolution is okay, provided that it is not atheistic Darwinian evolution. . . . They argue, of course, that such flexibility is necessary to get the creation idea into the public arena at all. However, it is also now becoming increasingly apparent that ID will never be allowed in the public schools. . . . And what good would it do anyhow? If the ID system has to be so diluted as to be acceptable to any religion or philosophy except raw atheism, then why bother?[75]

The problem with intelligent design is not with school systems that refuse to teach it or with courts that refuse to allow it when school boards try to put it in the biology curriculum. The problem is with intelligent design itself.

THE CENTRAL IMPORTANCE OF HUMAN ORIGINS

Darwinian theory is not beyond debate. It is a scientific theory, and efforts to fill in its gaps or to object to its structure should be addressed to the scientific community. Such efforts should be subject to the testing that marks the scientific enterprise. But the efforts to undermine Darwin in the public schools cannot be explained by the fact that evolutionary theory has gaps. There are no comparable efforts to insist that public school students learn about gaps in modern physics, such as the difficulty of reconciling general relativity and quantum mechanics.[76]

There are two major reasons that people care so deeply about evolution: it touches on human origins, and social Darwinism and eugenics have an unhappy history. Neither justifies the modern intelligent design movement, but both are worthy of attention in their own right.

Clearly, feelings run high on Darwin because his theories touch on human origins and human uniqueness. What is more surprising is that these feelings run high both for those who reject evolution and those who support it.[77] In *Fast Facts on False Teachings*, Ron Carlson and Ed Decker explain, from the anti-evolution perspective, exactly why the debate over human origins is so important. They contend that from the point of view of Darwin's theory "you are the descendant of a tiny cell of primordial protoplasm washed up on an empty beach three and a half billion years ago. . . . You are a mere grab-bag of atomic particles, a conglomeration of genetic substance. . . . [Y]ou came from nothing, you are going nowhere."[78] The Christian view, on the other hand, teaches us that "[y]ou are a special creation of a good and all-powerful God. You are the climax of His creation. . . . [Y]ou are unique. . . . Your Creator love[s] you."[79]

Of course, one response to Carlson and Decker is to say that it is just too bad if science reveals unflattering truths about human origins. This was the argument made by Clarence Darrow when he criticized a believer in the literal meaning of Genesis: "To make assertions not based on facts; to construct fantastic theories because he wants to dream; to entertain beliefs because he fears the truth shows only his craven fear of life and death."[80] But Darrow, a lawyer and an atheist, should not be taken as a reliable guide to the beliefs and motivations of scientists.[81] In fact, many scientists believe that scientific accounts of our origins, while they stand on a different empirical footing than traditional ones, serve the same purpose in giving us a positive account of our place in the world.

Consider, for example, the following passage from *The Future of Life* by the well-known modern evolutionary scientist E. O. Wilson:

Traced back far enough through time, across more than three billion years, all organisms on Earth share a common ancestry. That genetic unity is a fact-based history confirmed with increasing exactitude by the geneticists and paleontologists who reconstruct evolutionary genealogy. If *Homo sapiens* as a whole must have a creation myth—and emotionally in the age of globalization it seems we must—none is more solid and unifying for the species than evolutionary history.[82]

On this account, the theory of evolution is not something we must accept even if it displeases us. On the contrary, Wilson is arguing that globalization means that we are fortunate indeed that humans descended from a single source, rather than from two or three. In theory, scientists such as Wilson could do their work without bothering to think about such matters. But science is done by human beings, and scientists have long been eager to associate evolution with decidedly nonscientific ideas.

Wilson stresses unity while others stress progress,[83] but the desire to have science cast a positive light on the human endeavor is the same. The point is not just that evolutionary biologists, like everyone else, have a complex set of motivations for the work they do. The bigger point is that the matter of human origins is emotionally important to scientists in a way that other scientific theories are not. A simple thought experiment will show what I have in mind.

The Supreme Court's 1968 decision holding that Arkansas could not, for religious reasons, forbid the teaching of evolution did not require the state to teach that subject. As Justice Black noted in a concurrence, "It would be difficult to make a First Amendment case out of a state law eliminating the subject of higher mathematics, or astronomy, or biology from its curriculum."[84] Justice Stewart's concurring opinion made the same point.[85] Indeed, from a constitutional perspective, it is likely that a state could avoid the controversy over teaching human origins by simply teaching nothing on the subject in its public schools. Now imagine if the state of Arkansas actually took this step and eliminated biology from its public school curriculum. I confidently predict that scientists would be outraged. They would say that generations of youth would be condemned to dangerous ignorance, and those would be the mild speeches.

Yet where is the outrage among scientists over the fact that most American high school students do not study physics?[86] Surely physics is crucial for a modern scientific understanding of the world. Physics is, in fact, more fundamental than biology; physical reactions, after all, underlie the mechanism of evolution and of everything else in the science curriculum.[87] Although some scientists might argue that physics is too difficult for high schoolers, surely some of its basic ideas could be presented in an understandable manner. After all, public school biology classes hardly present a sophisticated view of their subject. On the other hand, when physics *is* taught in high school, where are the biblical literalists? Their protests are far weaker than they are when evolution is at stake, even though modern physics obviously challenges the biblical point of view.[88] Physicists reject the account in Joshua of the sun stopping in the sky, to give just one example.

If only sweet reason were involved, scientists and biblical literalists would be equally concerned about the study of physics as about the study of biology. But biology, with its closer connection to our sense of who we are, incites stronger reactions on both sides of the debate. The proof is in how people actually behave. Scientists rarely spend their time litigating against the government in federal court. Yet science teachers were among those challenging the ban on teaching evolution in Arkansas, the mandated teaching of creation science in Louisiana, and the inclusion of intelligent design in the biology curriculum in Pennsylvania. Biblical creationists are not the only ones who care deeply about their origins.

Evolution is not, of course, the first scientific theory to impinge on human pride. As everyone knows, there was once enormous controversy about the scientific evidence that the earth is not at the center of our solar system. But we care more about our own status than we do about the location of the planets and the stars. In fact, we seem to care more about our origins than about any other issue in biology.

In 2002, a suburban Atlanta public school system put stickers inside the covers of its high school biology textbooks. The stickers read: "This textbook contains material on evolution. Evolution is a theory, not a fact, regarding the origin of living things. This material should be approached with an open mind, studied carefully and critically considered."[89] A federal judge struck down the sticker requirement on the theory that it was designed to boost the religious theory of creationism.[90] An appellate court remanded the matter for further evidentiary hearings.[91] But step back from the controversy for a moment. Surely a biology text also casts doubt on the virgin birth. No one proposed a warning sticker on that issue.

Recognizing that we all care about where we came from may not resolve any immediate controversies, but perhaps it can lower the temperature over these disputes a bit. Neither scientists nor nonscientists are immune from feeling that we are special.

THE SHADOW OF EUGENICS

The second reason for the remarkable durability of disputes over evolution is the unhappy history of social Darwinism and eugenics. For some, by linking humans with other primates, Darwin's work opens up the possibility of oppressing or eliminating the poor in the name of progress. Social Darwinism followed in the wake of Darwin's publications. Building on Herbert Spencer's work, some political and social thinkers reasoned that the rich and powerful were the rightful winners in human history and that the poor and weak were doomed to die out.[92] Racist theories identified the good as white northern Europeans, and some social Darwinists were happy to give "progress" a push by supporting eugenic theories to weed out inferior races.[93] Sterilizations of people who were infirm were carried out in the United States, and the Nazis went much further.[94]

Early opponents of evolution, like William Jennings Bryan, were greatly concerned that teaching people about evolution would strengthen this social movement,[95] Some opponents of evolution today are troubled by the theory's past links to eugenics.[96] When John Thomas Scopes went on trial in 1925, Bryan never had an opportunity to present his closing argument to the jury in favor of convicting Scopes and upholding the Tennessee anti-evolution law.[97] Scopes's lawyer, Clarence Darrow, asked that the jury return a verdict of guilty because he was intent on challenging the law's validity on appeal.[98] But Bryan made his proposed closing argument public after the jury returned its guilty verdict, and the argument stressed what he saw as the social dangers of Darwin. Bryan argued that the study of evolution undermined love of others and discouraged efforts to improve society.[99]

But opposition to social Darwinism should not lead us to attack Darwin. We understand today that social Darwinism is a political theory that is not part of the scientific theory of evolution. Darwinian evolution does not tell us how to shape our culture. We can invent eyeglasses and thus remove poor eyesight from the survival equation. We can help the poor as we see fit. Darwin's ideas do not tell us how we should treat each other. Indeed, even at the level of nonhuman organisms, Darwinian evolution says nothing about the superiority of those that survive. If external conditions change, once-successful species can die out, as happened to the dinosaurs and many others.

Of course, any theory, scientific or otherwise, can be cynically misused in favor of the rich and powerful. There are religious people who argue that God made rich and poor alike and who are less than enthusiastic about efforts to reduce poverty. It is not a sensible strategy to oppose a scientific theory because it can be misused. A clever student can use a chemistry textbook to figure out how to build a bomb, but few would ban the teaching of chemistry as a result.

Still, vigilance is sensible in this field. If scientists claim that Darwin tells us how to live our lives, they should be called to account. Science tells us how the world is, not how it ought to be.[100] We are responsible for living ethical lives, an endeavor where religion can be invaluable. And we would be wise to retain a sense of humility, an attribute often found in traditional faith and often forgotten by scientists.[101]

In the closing statement that Bryan never delivered to the jury in the Scopes case, he offered some useful observations on the limits of science:

Science is a magnificent force, but it is not a teacher of morals. It can perfect machinery, but it adds no moral restraints to protect society from the misuse of the machine. It can also build gigantic intellectual ships, but it constructs no moral rudders for the control of the storm tossed human vessel.[102]

THE ARGUMENT FROM DESIGN

The modern intelligent design movement is a disfigured product of biblical literalism and federal court litigation. It stems, however, from an ancient and more serious religious enterprise. It is a version of the venerable argument from design. The original argument from design is an argument for the existence of God. The modern intelligent design movement pretends it has nothing to do with God, because it is trying to force itself into the public school science curriculum. If we put the modern diversion aside and look at the original argument from design, we will see ideas still worth considering, ideas that are lost when watered-down religion is forced into the public square. The argument from design is a religious argument, and thus should not be taught in public school science classes. But it can be studied with profit in countless other settings, and it still serves, directly or indirectly, to influence millions.

This important argument received its most thorough early explication in the work of Saint Thomas Aquinas, the great thirteenth-century philosopher and theologian.[103] In his classic *Summa Theologica*, Aquinas presented five proofs for the existence of God, the fifth of which is the argument from design. The five proofs, in summary form, proceed as follows.[104] First, some things are in motion, and therefore they must have been moved by another. The first mover, the one that is not moved by another, is God. Second, some things are caused, and the first cause is God. Third, contingent beings at some point fail to exist. Yet not everything fails to exist. Thus, there is a necessary being, which is God. Fourth, some things are greater than others, but for greatness to be meaningful, there must be a greatest being, which is God. And finally, we have the argument from design, in Aquinas's words:

We see that things which lack intelligence, such as natural bodies, act for an end, and this is evident from their acting always, or nearly always, in the same way. . . . Hence it is plain that not fortuitously, but designedly, do they achieve their end. Now whatever lacks intelligence cannot move towards an end, unless it be directed by some being endowed with knowledge and intelligence; as the arrow is shot to its mark by the archer. Therefore some intelligent being exists by whom all natural things are directed to their end; and this being we call God.[105]

Whatever one makes of these arguments, they are not about the inconsequential "God of the gaps" of the modern intelligent design movement. These are classic attempts to make sense of large questions concerning our very existence. And Aquinas's arguments put no arbitrary limit on the efforts of science to explain natural phenomena.

When Darwin began his work in the mid-nineteenth century, the most popular version of the argument from design was that put forward by the Reverend William Paley in his 1802 book *Natural Theology*.[106] Paley was reacting in part to pre-Darwinian versions of evolutionary theory as well as to other sources of what he called the "scepticism" concerning God's existence "with which the present times are charged."[107] He began his book with a famous version of the argument from design:

> In crossing a heath, suppose I pitched my foot against a stone, and were asked how the stone came to be there, I might possibly answer that, for any thing I knew to the contrary, it had lain there for ever. . . . But suppose I had found a watch upon the ground, and it should be enquired how the watch happened to be in that place. . . . [W]hen we came to inspect the watch, we perceive, (what we could not discover in the stone,) that its several parts are framed and put together for a purpose. . . . [T]he inference, we think, is inevitable; that watch must have had a maker.[108]

Paley argued that the many elaborate structures we see around us show that God is the watchmaker of the world. When Darwin was at Cambridge University, he studied Paley with great pleasure. Indeed, Darwin wrote in his *Autobiography*:

> I am convinced that I could have written out the whole of [Paley's 1794 book] *Evidences* with perfect correctness. . . . [T]he logic of this book and as I may add of his *Natural Theology* gave me as much delight as did Euclid. The careful study of these works . . . was the only part of the Academical Course which, as I then felt and as I still believe, was the most use to me in the education of my mind.[109]

Darwin's theory of evolution was, in part, an effort to answer Paley's question about how complex structures can come about. With biological organisms, Darwin showed that it was not necessary to have an intelligent agent to bring about each change. Natural selection acting on random mutations in particular environments can account for what we observe.

When Darwin's theory is looked at from this perspective, it is clear why the theory is not an argument that God does not exist. Darwin was not concerned with how the first living organism emerged, still less with how the universe itself came into existence. So after Darwin, the existence of the DNA that made evolution possible and of the earth on which we live still leads some to the argument from design.[110] Moreover, Darwin was doing science, so he was not concerned with nonfalsifiable aspects of religious faith, such as questions of the soul or the afterlife, or whether evolution itself was the creation of God.

It is also clear from this perspective what the traditional argument from design does and does not do. It attempts to persuade us that God created the world, an effort that some find persuasive after Darwin, and that some do not. Even if you fully believe in the argument from design, it does not tell you whether to be a Christian or whether to believe in a divine moral code.[111] Revelation and faith are central to questions of that type.

The modern intelligent design movement does not clarify anything or inspire anyone. It is an odd version of the argument from design, crippled by pretending to be science and by pretending that evolution is inconsistent with faith.

MODERN SCIENCE AND THE
ORDER OF THE UNIVERSE

If you want to get a sense of modern thinkers who are inspired to sweeping ideas about the universe, put aside creation science and intelligent design and read accounts of modern mainstream physics. It is an extraordinary testament to the lifeless religion surrounding us today that there is more inspiration to be found in the science section of a bookstore than in the religion section. I want to explain the faith in an orderly and beautiful universe expressed by many modern physicists. But before I do so, some caveats are in order.

First of all, I am not talking about the conventional religious beliefs of these scientists. Some have traditional Catholic, Protestant, Jewish, or other religious faiths, and some do not. Moreover, scientists' faith in a comprehensible and comprehensive theory of physics does not tell them or us how to live our lives, nor does it answer many of the other questions religion addresses. Finally, these physicists are not believers in the modern intelligent design movement, and they are typically not following Aquinas's argument from design.

The first point is obvious: modern intelligent design is a confused religious attack on Darwin, which is hardly likely to appeal to a physicist seeking a grand, unified theory. The second point is less obvious. When a scientist says he believes there is an order in the universe or that he is learning about God by learning about the cosmos, the scientist may not be focusing on God as the creator of the universe but rather on a God who is identical with or embodied in the universe itself. In other words, the scientist may be expressing not a transcendent faith but an immanent one.

But none of this should obscure the big picture. Many modern physicists are closer to the spirituality millions have felt from Aquinas to the present than are the members of the school board who brought intelligent design to Dover, Pennsylvania. Although not all present-day physicists are inspired by a belief in a comprehensible universe, a surprising number are.

So let us look at these beliefs that inspire so many modern thinkers. These ideas should not be taught in a public school science class any more than Genesis should be. But limiting ourselves to the subject matter of ninth-grade biology is hardly the way to appreciate our place in the universe.

EINSTEIN'S GOD

In the 1920s, experimental confirmations of his theory of relativity made Albert Einstein world famous. In 1929, for reasons that are unclear, Boston's Cardinal O'Connell called Einstein's theory "befogged speculation" that raised "the ghastly apparition of atheism."[112] A rabbi, knowing that Einstein was Jewish, sent him a telegram asking, "Do you believe in

God?" Einstein replied, "I believe in Spinoza's God, Who reveals Himself in the lawful harmony of the world, not in a God Who concerns Himself with the fate and the doings of mankind."[113]

Albert Einstein's God was not the traditional Jewish God, but rather a God, as Einstein wrote elsewhere, "who reveals himself in all that exists."[114] Einstein looked to this intuitive sense of the order of the universe when he rejected the quantum theory, saying "God does not play dice with the universe."[115] He believed deeply that the laws of the universe were, in the end, simple enough to be understandable to humankind. When asked near the end of his life how he would feel if those laws turned out not to be so simple, he replied, "Then I would not be interested in them."[116]

The appeal of Einstein's God to modern scientists is nothing short of remarkable. Evolutionary biologist Richard Dawkins, an avowed atheist who attacks religion relentlessly,[117] explicitly says, "I too am religious," if by religious we use Einstein's definition: "To sense that behind anything that can be experienced there is a something that our mind cannot grasp and whose beauty and sublimity reaches us only indirectly and as a feeble reflection."[118]

So it is certainly worth our while to get a sense of Einstein's God. In order to do that, let us look for a moment at Baruch Spinoza, the seventeenth-century Dutch Jewish philosopher Einstein cited in his 1929 telegram. Many modern scientists find Spinoza's ideas attractive.[119] This includes those scientists who, unlike Einstein, accept the fundamentally probabilistic account of nature given by quantum theory. Indeed, Niels Bohr, a founder of that theory, used to playfully argue with Einstein about whether Spinoza would have accepted quantum theory.[120]

Baruch Spinoza identified God with nature. He referred repeatedly to "God or Nature" throughout his most important philosophical work. More precisely, he identified God with the fundamental laws of nature.[121] To Spinoza, everything we experience, whether it is the movement of the planets, the comings and goings of our friends, or our hopes and fears, is the result of antecedent causes. In other words, everything has a cause, even our thoughts. In this deterministic universe, humans have the ability, through the exercise of reason, to understand these causes and thus make sense of the universe.[122]

Spinoza's God, as a result, is not like a mighty person somewhere in the heavens. That image is far too anthropomorphic for the philosopher. As Spinoza wrote in a letter explaining why he declined to assign human attributes to God, "I believe that, if a triangle could speak, it would say, in like manner, that God is eminently triangular, while a circle would say that the divine nature is eminently circular."[123] As a consequence, Spinoza's God is not a judge who determines if individual people are rewarded or punished.[124] Judging, after all, is a human occupation.

These ideas, along with his other objections to traditional religion, were sufficiently heretical in the seventeenth century to get Spinoza excommunicated from the Jewish community in which he had been raised and to prevent him from publishing his work under his own name for fear of retribution from the Christian majority.[125] Not until many years after his death was Spinoza openly studied and cited by major philosophers.[126]

To this day, it is difficult to label Spinoza in terms of religious belief. To some, he is a pantheist, to others an atheist, and yet the German poet Novalis famously described him as a "God-intoxicated Man."[127] It is, in fact, hard to think of another philosopher who refers to God as often as Spinoza does. In any event, it is easy to see why Spinoza appeals to many modern scientists. The idea of an orderly universe that can be analyzed by human beings is obviously attractive to them. Always popular with physicists, Spinoza has recently been cited as a major influence by neuroscientists such as Antonio Damasio.[128]

THE FAITH OF MODERN SCIENTISTS

At a deep level, scientists need a kind of faith to keep doing their work. In theory, every morning when she wakes up a scientist could question all of her assumptions about the universe, including whether it exists outside her thoughts and whether its laws are the same today as they were yesterday. In practice, no one works that way. Scientists need to believe not only that the universe has laws but that we can figure them out and test them. There are countless philosophers and skeptics of all stripes who question those assumptions, but they are not in the lab doing science.

Consider the quest by modern physicists to develop a grand unified theory that would bring together relativity and quantum theory. At present, relativity gives the best account of gravity, whereas quantum theory is at the root of our understanding of all of the other forces physicists find in the universe. But these two approaches are fundamentally different—in particular, relativity does not embody a probabilistic point of view.[129] Scientists have worked for decades to try to bring these two theories together into a unified, mathematical whole. An approach known as superstring theory is one of the leading candidates to do this, and superstring theorists are convinced they will succeed.[130] They are optimistic because, as one of them, Cumrun Vafa, has written, their theory "is the most beautiful and consistent structure we have."[131] This optimism is shared by another leading theorist, Lisa Randall, who says of upcoming experiments that they "will tell us about the nature of matter at distances smaller than any physical process ever observed. At high energies, truths about the universe should start to explode. Secrets of the cosmos will begin to unravel. I for one can't wait."[132] The best explanation for this upbeat perspective—a point of view that is indispensable for actually doing research—is that offered by superstring theorist Brian Greene, who wrote, "With solid faith that laws of the large and the small should fit together into a coherent whole, physicists are relentlessly hunting down the elusive unified theory."[133] The key word here is *faith*.

My point is not that the religious and philosophical beliefs of superstring theorists should be taught in public school physics classes. It is the opposite. It is exhilarating to hear voices talking openly about their belief in the beautiful structure of the cosmos. Let these voices be heard in the private sphere and in philosophy and theology classrooms. If people of faith would step back from the counterproductive effort to mangle religion into intelligent design so that it can be crammed into the public schools, they too could present their real beliefs more clearly. They too could be heard in the private sphere and in philosophy and theology classrooms. For some religious people, the God who created the universe and the beautiful universe he created might bear some resemblance—maybe even a close resemblance—to the God or Nature that some scientists seek. For others, there would be fundamental, unbridgeable differences. But for everyone, religion and faith could take their real place in American life.

The biggest threat to modern religion does not come from science. Indeed, it is often scientists who express spiritual ideas in their writings. The biggest threat comes from those who would degrade religion until it can be placed—unrecognizable and unattractive—in the public schools.

CHAPTER 4

The Ultimate Demise of
Christmas and Chanukah

MINISTERS HAVE BEMOANED the commercialization of Christmas in America since the nineteenth century. Jewish leaders have complained almost as long about how Chanukah has been distorted by its proximity to Christmas. But it has fallen to our generation to bring about the ultimate insult to these holidays.

Today, Christmas has become so devoid of meaning that Santa Claus and Christmas trees are displayed by merchants in Muslim countries where proselytizing by Christians is a crime, yet Christian spokespeople in America present this use of Santa and the tree as a model to be emulated. After all, the great battle over Christmas in our time is not to put Christ back into Christmas but to put Christmas into Wal-Mart.

Chanukah, a minor Jewish holiday, has long been inflated in importance so that Jewish children would not feel left out when their Christian friends got presents on Christmas. Now Chanukah has not only overshadowed other Jewish holidays but has also overshadowed the central emblem of Judaism: the menorah. The historic seven-branched Temple menorah has been replaced in Jewish consciousness by the very different and less important Chanukah menorah.

With the Ten Commandments and intelligent design, we saw how efforts to push religion into the public square tended to drain religious teachings of their meaning and to distort those teachings in troubling ways. With the celebration of Christmas and Chanukah the story begins the same way, so we will start by looking at the litigation over Christmas and Chanukah symbols on courthouse steps and other public property. Here, as with the Ten Commandments, we will see legal battles where victory is more dangerous than defeat. Religion, in order to win the dubious honor of appearing on the lawn of city hall, must be stripped of its real meaning.

But Christmas and Chanukah have long had commercial potential far beyond the Ten Commandments and intelligent design. So we will continue by looking at how the economic side of these holidays, combined with the battles over the public square, have resulted in a remarkable victory for the commercialization of religion. The true history and meaning of both Christmas and Chanukah have become changed almost beyond recognition.

THE FRACTURED LEGAL LANDSCAPE

When the Supreme Court, in cases involving the posting of the Ten Commandments in public spaces, presented a bewildering variety of opinions and tests, it was simply following the path it had laid out in earlier cases involving holiday displays. And the result is the same: the law is plagued with uncertainty and inconsistency as local officials try to figure out when a display is sufficiently secular to be allowed. The only thing that is clear is that for a display to be upheld, it must be devoid of any meaningful religious content.[1]

The Supreme Court first became involved in the area in 1984 when it considered the constitutionality of a Christmas display erected by the city of Pawtucket, Rhode Island.[2] For more than forty years, the city had, in cooperation with downtown retail merchants, put up a display in a park. Challengers argued that the inclusion in the display of a crèche—a tableau of figures representing the infant Jesus, Mary, and Joseph at the time of Jesus' birth—constituted an establishment of religion. The Supreme Court divided 5–4 in upholding the display. In his opinion for the majority, Chief Justice Burger began by noting that the display included not just the crèche, which he described as a "Christian symbol," but "many of the figures and decorations traditionally associated with Christmas, including, among other things, a Santa Claus house, reindeer pulling Santa's sleigh, candy-striped poles, a Christmas tree, carolers, cut-out figures representing such characters as a clown, an elephant, and a teddy bear, hundreds of colored lights, [and] a large banner that reads 'SEASONS GREETINGS.'"[3]

Having thus set the stage, Chief Justice Burger upheld the display on several grounds. He began by noting the long history in the United States of recognition by the government of the importance of religion as well as the absence of controversy over the Pawtucket display for more than forty years.[4] Burger then made the familiar point that a religious motivation on the part of legislators—such as the desire to outlaw theft because it contravenes the Ten Commandments—does not void a law if it serves nonreligious values as well.[5] Here, although the crèche may have been included in part for religious reasons, the entire display serves secular purposes as well because it helps "celebrate the Holiday and . . . depict the origins of that Holiday" and it "engenders a friendly community spirit of goodwill in keeping with the season."[6]

Justice O'Connor concurred, emphasizing the endorsement test that she pioneered and that others follow. She found that a reasonable observer of the entire display would not find that "the government intends to endorse the Christian beliefs represented by the crèche. Instead, this observer would find that the "display celebrates a public holiday. . . . The holiday itself has very strong secular components and traditions. . . . The crèche is a traditional symbol of the holiday that is very commonly displayed along with purely secular symbols, as it was in Pawtucket."[8]

The dissenting justices believed that Pawtucket included the crèche in the display for religious purposes only. Pawtucket argued that it sought "only to participate in the celebration of a national holiday and to attract people to the downtown area in order to promote pre-Christmas retail sales and to help engender the spirit of goodwill and neighborliness commonly associated with the Christmas season," but the dissenters believed these purposes could have been achieved with a display limited to secular symbols such as "Santa Claus [and] reindeer."[9]

The reaction to this decision was just what you would expect. Some noted that Christmas displays were being upheld at the cost of removing their religious content and that Pawtucket was strengthening the powerful bond between Christmas and shopping.[10] Others were delighted that a crèche could be part of a public display.[11] The group most unhappy with the decision was the group that had to live with its consequences: lower court judges. Lawyers on all sides quickly became aware that municipal Christmas displays would be judged by their array of symbols. Judges had to sort all of this out.

Usually, lower court judges are quite deferential to the Supreme Court. But grappling with post-Pawtucket litigation was too much for some of them. One judge criticized the "'St. Nicholas too' test—a city can get by with displaying a crèche if it throws in a sleigh full of toys and a Santa Claus, too."[12] Another judge opined that the Supreme Court was "requiring scrutiny more commonly associated with interior decorators than with the judiciary."[13]

When the Supreme Court decided two more cases on holiday displays in 1989, many observers hoped that the situation might be clarified. Instead, it got worse. The cases involved two recurring holiday displays on public property in Pittsburgh. In one, a crèche was placed on the main staircase of the Allegheny County Courthouse. In the other, a Christmas tree, a Chanukah menorah, and a sign saluting liberty were placed outside the City-County Building. The first display was struck down, but the second was allowed.[14]

Four justices, led by Justice Kennedy, would have upheld both displays.[15] Kennedy emphasized his coercion test, as he later did in the Ten Commandments cases. For Kennedy, these displays on government property did not force anyone to do anything: "Passersby who disagree with the message conveyed by these displays are free to ignore them."[16] Kennedy sharply criticized the endorsement test, arguing that it was difficult to apply and that any number of governmental recognitions of religion, such as a presidential proclamation that thanks God or a prayer by a legislative chaplain could be said to endorse religion.[17] Kennedy also rejected the secular purpose test as too hostile to religion.[18]

Kennedy and those who joined him made clear that a purely religious symbol, such as the crèche, could be placed on public property during Christmas without any constitutional problem.[19] But Kennedy candidly stated that his approach required "difficult line drawing" in some cases, and he noted two instances where he thought a religious display would be unconstitutional:

I doubt not, for example, that the [Establishment] Clause forbids a city to permit the permanent erection of a large Latin cross on the roof of city hall. . . . [This] would place the government's weight behind an obvious effort to proselytize on behalf of a particular religion. . . . [I]f a city chose to recognize, through religious displays, every significant Christian holiday while ignoring the holidays of all other faiths, the argument that the city was simply recognizing certain holidays celebrated by its citizens without . . . applying pressure to obtain adherents would be . . . difficult to maintain."[20]

Three justices, led by Justice Stevens, would have struck down both the unadorned crèche and the Christmas tree–menorah display. Just as the four led by Kennedy would uphold most displays, the Stevens group felt the Establishment Clause created "a strong presumption against the display of religious symbols on public property."[21] They believed that the Pittsburgh displays had the purpose of advancing religion and that they spurred divisions in the society.[22]

But Justice Stevens's position, like that of Justice Kennedy, did not avoid line-drawing problems. Stevens noted two religious symbols he and his like-minded colleagues would permit. Carvings on a courtroom wall could depict Moses, Confucius, and Mohammed if they were surrounded by secular figures such as William Blackstone and John Marshall since that would signal "respect not for great proselytizers but for great lawgivers . . . [and] it would be absurd . . . to exclude religious paintings by Italian Renaissance masters from a public museum."[23]

Only two justices, Blackmun and O'Connor, distinguished between the two displays. Because of their swing votes, the crèche on the courthouse steps was struck down, and the Christmas tree–menorah display in front of the government office building was upheld. The former display was seen as improperly endorsing religion, while the Christmas tree–menorah display along with the sign saluting liberty "sends a message of pluralism and freedom to choose one's own beliefs."[24] These justices, unlike Kennedy and Stevens, did not defend a strong presumption either for or against religious displays on public property, preferring instead "case-specific examinations of the challenged government action."[25]

Since the Pittsburgh cases, the lower courts have been pretty much on their own. In many towns with Christmas displays, either a consensus has been reached on a set of symbols, or interested parties lack the means to litigate, so the matter stays out of court. However, when consensus is not reached and a lawsuit results, it is hard to predict the outcome.

Because the Supreme Court has not resolved any holiday display cases since the Pittsburgh cases, and because the Court's later Ten Commandments decisions are even more confusing, lower courts examine the entire context of the display before them and apply some combination of history, secular purpose, endorsement, coercion, potential for divisiveness, and whatever other approaches they believe the Supreme Court would use.

Clearly, there is not going to be a definitive judicial consensus in this area in the foreseeable future. A series of appointments creating a more solidly conservative or solidly liberal Supreme Court might move the line somewhat, but line drawing will remain the central reality. Will liberal justices allow explicitly religious pictures of the infant Jesus in the courthouse lobby if the pictures are copies of "Renaissance masters"? Will conservative justices allow a sign in that lobby saying "Christmas marks the birth of the son of God," since it does not coerce observance and taxpayers "are free to ignore" the message? That judicial appointments will someday resolve this matter is wishful thinking. Recall that even Justice Kennedy, the staunchest advocate of religious displays, would not accept a jurisdiction marking every significant Christian holiday while ignoring those of other faiths. Think about how broad the phrase "other faiths" is in America.

Thus, believing that holiday displays in the public square will reinforce meaningful religious belief is also wishful thinking. Such displays will always represent a compromise among existing groups in the population along with steps taken to shape the displays in anticipation of litigation. There simply is no public consensus in this area, which is hardly surprising given American pluralism. Jewish groups are divided on whether putting a menorah alongside a Christmas tree is good policy.[26] Does it enhance a real sense of Jewish identity or diminish it? Some Christians believe that the crèche is diminished when it is displayed along with non-Christian or secular symbols in a holiday display.[27] And, of course, millions of religious Americans are neither Christian nor Jewish. They have to decide whether to try to push their own symbols into the holiday display mix, with all of the costs that entails.

Under the circumstances, holiday religious displays will hardly serve as a meaningful counterweight to the commercial nature of the season. Indeed, they often end up supporting commercialism. For this reason, railing at the Supreme Court's divided opinions is understandable but in the long run has little to do with the actual substance of religion in America. It would be useful if the Court could come together on an approach that would provide more clear guidance to local governments and to lower courts. It would lower the cost of litigation and might lower temperatures a bit. But it would not change the reality that in a country as diverse as ours, with our twin traditions of free exercise and non-establishment, putting Christmas and Chanukah on the courthouse steps is not good news for either holiday.

Let us look briefly at just two of the Christmas cases that have been litigated since the Supreme Court last spoke on the matter. These two cases have a good deal in common: the factual and legal inquiries were difficult, the judges involved ended up divided among themselves, and the Supreme Court did not get involved. In one case, the display was upheld; in the other, it was initially struck down before being upheld a few years later. I doubt that many people would argue that the various judges' opinions in these cases were consistent with each other. More important, I am convinced that in neither case was the cost of getting religion into the public square worth the prize.

The first case arose in the Village of Waunakee, Wisconsin, a town of about six thousand.[28] For roughly forty years, the village put up a Christmas display in a park, usually from late November to early January. Apparently the display was largely devoted to a crèche. After receiving complaints in the 1990s, the village modified the display so that the crèche was surrounded by lighted evergreen trees, a flagpole decorated with lights, and a sign reading, "During the Holiday Season, the Village of Waunakee salutes liberty. Let these festive lights and times remind us that we are the keepers of the flame of liberty and our legacy of freedom. Whatever your religion or beliefs, enjoy the holidays—Waunakee Village Board."[29]

A lawsuit was brought arguing that the new display violated the Establishment Clause, and the case reached the Supreme Court of Wisconsin in 1994. The court upheld the display in an opinion by Justice Day, over a dissent written by Chief Justice Heffernan and joined by one of his colleagues.

Justice Day noted that the Waunakee display had some similarities to the Pawtucket, Rhode Island, display upheld by the United States Supreme Court. In both cases, the display had been put up for about forty years without inciting controversy, and in both cases the display consisted of a crèche surrounded by more secular symbols.[30] Justice Day's opinion for his court then turned to the United States Supreme Court decisions that arose out of the two displays in Pittsburgh. Day noted that under Justice Kennedy's view for four justices, the Waunakee display would clearly be upheld since those four justices would have upheld the crèche standing alone on government property.[31] Day then argued that Justice O'Connor, one of the swing voters in the Pittsburgh cases, would have upheld the Waunakee display because, even though she would not allow a crèche standing alone, she placed weight on the sign saluting liberty as a basis for allowing the combined Christmas tree–Menorah display.[32] A similar sign was present in Waunakee.

Chief Justice Heffernan's dissent found that the display violated a religious freedom provision in the Wisconsin Constitution, but it is reasonably clear that he would have found that it violated the United States Constitution, as interpreted in the Pawtucket and Pittsburgh cases, as well.[33] Heffernan emphasized that the crèche "is a religious symbol portraying an event central to the Christian faith. Christians believe that God sent his son, Jesus Christ, into the world to be the Savior. . . . The crèche is a symbol of Christ's birth and has no secular connotations."[34] Echoing Justice O'Connor's endorsement test, Heffernan then argued that residents of Waunakee who are not Christian "are placed in the position of outsiders when the government pays homage to Christian symbols."[35] He maintained that the crèche negated the secular aspects of the lighted trees and the sign; indeed, he contended that "if the village government really wished to 'remind us that we are the keepers of the flame of liberty and [our] legacy of freedom,' they would not limit the display to one religion's symbols."[36]

In December 1994, just a few months after the Wisconsin Supreme Court upheld the Village of Waunakee display, litigation began on a similar question in New Jersey. This time an appellate court struck down the display, although a few years later another panel of the same court upheld it.

In 1994, the City of Jersey City, New Jersey, mounted the holiday display in question on the lawn in front of city hall as it had in the past.[37] This display consisted of a crèche on one side of the main entrance and a menorah on the other. The city also decorated an evergreen tree on the lawn with lights and Christmas ornaments. Finally, on December 16, 1994, after receiving complaints, the city erected a sign next to its display reading, "Through this display and others throughout the year, the City of Jersey City is pleased to celebrate the diverse cultural and ethnic heritages of its peoples."[38]

A few days later, a lawsuit was filed challenging the display. In November 1995, a federal district court judge ruled that the display violated the Establishment Clause of the United States Constitution and issued an injunction saying it could not be put up again.[39] Then matters veered toward the bizarre.

Rather than appeal the district court order, Jersey City decided to modify its display by keeping all of the original elements but adding several new figures, including a four-foot-tall plastic Santa Claus, a four-foot-tall plastic Frosty the Snowman, and a red wooden sled.[40] The challengers went back to the district court, which upheld the new display, saying: "I conclude that by making these additions defendants have sufficiently demystified the [holy], they have sufficiently desanctified sacred symbols, and they have sufficiently deconsecrated the sacred to escape the confines of the injunctive order in this case."[41] The district court also ruled that if Santa, Frosty, and/or the sled were stolen or destroyed, they had to be replaced within twenty-four hours.[42]

Before continuing with this saga, it is worth stepping back for a moment. Only in America can a plastic Frosty the Snowman wield such power. If kidnapped for a single day, Frosty's demystifying power is lost. It is hard to believe anyone on either side of the issue is happy about any of this.

On appeal, the United States Court of Appeals for the Third Circuit reversed the district court, finding that it had not provided an adequate justification that Jersey City's display was constitutional.[43] Judge Lewis's opinion for the court went through the Supreme Court precedents and concluded that the court would not find that the crèche and the menorah were sufficiently secularized by the other elements of the display, such as Santa and Frosty.[44] One of Lewis's colleagues concurred, using a slightly different analysis of the precedents to reach the same conclusion.[45]

When Jersey City sought review in the United States Supreme Court, that Court declined to hear the case, after which litigation continued to see if the district court could find an adequate basis for upholding the display.[46] The Supreme Court's denying review does not mean it agrees with the lower court decision before it. It only indicates that the justices did not believe the case sufficiently important to warrant their attention. No one sought United States Supreme Court review of the Village of Waunakee decision, but if anyone had, it is quite likely the Court would have declined to hear that case as well. To put it politely, the Supreme Court is not eager to enter this thicket every time a lower court has to decide the legality of a Christmas display. The Court itself is likely to end up deeply divided in every such case.

It might be possible to reconcile Justice Day's opinion in the Waunakee case with Judge Lewis's approach to the Jersey City display. Maybe the content of the sign in Waunakee played a key role, or perhaps Jersey City was not able to call upon quite as long a tradition of city holiday displays as the Wisconsin village was. But there have been many such cases in the lower courts, and the more honest analysis is that courts are understandably reaching inconsistent decisions in many settings because there is no clear legal guidance coming from the Supreme Court.[47]

In fact, when the Jersey City display, complete with Frosty and his friends, came back before the courts, the result changed. Recall that Judge Lewis had only held that the city had not provided an adequate justification for its actions. The city, back before the district court after the Supreme Court's decision not to take the case, argued that a proper reading of emerging Supreme Court precedent made the display constitutional. The district court ruled against Jersey City, and the matter went once again to the United States Court of Appeals for the Third Circuit, where it was heard by a new panel of judges.[48] This time the opinion for the appellate court was written by Samuel Alito, who is now a member of the United States Supreme Court. Judge Alito affirmed the district court holding that the original Jersey City display—the one that lacked secular elements—was unconstitutional, but he concluded, over a dissent by Judge Nygaard, that the new display, which included the various secular plastic figures, was lawful.[49] Frosty the Snowman was back on the job.

The judicial doctrine here is incoherent. But one thing is clear: a truly religious display on public property conveying the central meaning of Christ's birth to Christians would not be upheld in the courts. Only if the display secularizes the holiday does it have a chance of passing muster.

THE SPEAKERS' CORNER ALTERNATIVE

Of course, truly religious displays are allowed on private property, including homes and church property, and millions of such displays are visible during Christmas and throughout the year all over the United States. Nonetheless, as the litigation in Pawtucket, Pittsburgh, Waunakee, Jersey City, and elsewhere suggests, there is a strong effort to put some kind of Christmas message into the public square.

There is an alternative way of doing this that deserves mention. I do not believe that, in the end, it can achieve the goals of those who want real religion in public places, but it is worth looking at. In 1995, six years after the Supreme Court struck down the crèche on the courthouse steps in Pittsburgh, the Court upheld the holiday display of a cross in Capitol Square, a ten-acre, state-owned plaza surrounding the Columbus, Ohio, statehouse.[50] Moreover, seven justices agreed with this result. To understand what is going on here, let us look at the idea of the public forum.

Some government properties, such as sidewalks, are regarded by the courts as public forums. People are free to speak their mind in these settings, even if what they say displeases the government. Although the government can regulate the time, place, and manner of speech in order to avoid problems like excess noise or dangerous crowding, it cannot discriminate on the basis of the speaker's point of view. So it would be obviously unconstitutional for the government to say that you can criticize Republicans but not Democrats when you are walking down the street.[51]

Freedom of speech under the United States Constitution includes the freedom to engage in religious speech, and here, too, the government cannot discriminate. If Christians can preach in a public forum, Muslims can as well.[52] One of the best-known examples of the public forum idea came about in 1872 when legislation in Great Britain made possible the creation of Speakers' Corner in the northeast quadrant of Hyde Park in London.[53] To this day, any visitor to Speakers' Corner confronts a free-for-all of speaking and preaching representing an astonishing range of views, and any visitor who chooses can join right in.[54]

There is an enormous body of law in the United States on which areas qualify as public forums: what sorts of activities, such as picketing, are allowed there; whether the government can create a licensing system for use of the forum to meet its legitimate needs; and so on. From our perspective, a modern series of cases concerning the rights of religious groups to use public settings turns out to be relevant to the question of holiday displays. Lawyers sometimes use phrases like "limited public forum" to describe a setting where the government was under no obligation to allow speech but affirmatively chose to do so. In such places, once it has created the forum, the government cannot discriminate on the basis of the speaker's viewpoint.

In 1981, the Court considered the policy of the University of Missouri at Kansas City, a public institution, on the use of school facilities.[55] The university provided rooms where more than one hundred student groups could hold meetings. It declined, however, to provide space to a Christian student group, fearing that to do so would constitute an establishment of religion. When the Christian group sued, the United States Supreme Court, by a vote of 8–1, said that the university had to provide them with a room.[56] Not to do so was improper discrimination in the running of a limited public forum. Outsiders would not think that the university was supporting Christianity any more than it was supporting any of the political groups that already used school facilities.[57]

The Court later applied the principle in 1993 when it ruled that if a public school board allowed civic groups to use school property after hours for programs that could include matters such as advice on child rearing, it could not bar a religious group that wanted to present a program on Christian family values.[58] Every member of the Supreme Court agreed with this result.

In 2001, the Supreme Court applied these principles to a New York public elementary school that allowed after-hours use of its facilities for programs, such as the Boy Scouts, that encouraged moral values.[59] The Court concluded that the school could not bar the Good News Club, a Christian group that presented programs including Bible study and prayer for children ages six through twelve.[60] Three justices dissented because of concerns that this type of use links the state too closely with religion.[61]

The lesson of these cases is that public schools are free to prevent outside groups from using their facilities, but if they open up those facilities, they cannot discriminate against religious viewpoints. While this line of cases was being decided, the Christmas display of a cross came before the Court.

For over a century, Capitol Square in Columbus, Ohio, has been used for speeches and gatherings, religious and secular, on a variety of topics and causes.[62] Under Ohio law, the square is available "for use by the public . . . for free discussion of public questions, or for activities of a broad public purpose."[63] Ohio has often allowed unattended displays on Capitol Square, including a Christmas tree, a Chanukah menorah, and exhibits during an arts festival. In November 1993, the state received an application from a private group to place a large cross on the square during the Christmas season. Appended to the foot of the cross was a relatively small disclaimer stating that "this cross was erected by private individuals without government support for the purpose of expressing respect for the holiday season."[64]

The application was refused on the ground that a cross in front of the Ohio State Capitol would constitute an establishment of religion. Observers would see the cross in front of the Capitol and perceive an improper connection between them.[65] The case reached the Supreme Court, which held that putting up the cross in this public forum would not constitute an establishment of religion.[66] The seven justices who voted to uphold the display agreed that this result followed from the public school access cases it had previously decided.[67] Ohio here is in the position of the University of Missouri at Kansas City. Once it had opened up a public forum, it could not discriminate against this religious symbol.

Beyond that point, however, these justices were divided. Justices O'Connor, Souter, and Breyer considered it important to determine if a reasonable observer would believe that Ohio was endorsing Christianity. They concluded that the case was close and that a larger disclaimer might have been desirable, but given the long history of this public forum, the reasonable observer would understand that this was private speech.[68] The other four justices in the majority—Scalia, Thomas, Kennedy, and Chief Justice Rehnquist—did not consider the endorsement test relevant. No religious symbol, no matter how it was perceived, would constitute an establishment of religion in this public forum.[69] For Justices Stevens and Ginsburg, who dissented, the public forum did not change the fact that this use of state property was an establishment of religion. For Ginsburg, a larger disclaimer, visible at a distance, or a large permanent marker erected by the state indicating that displays did not represent the government's views might have made a difference, but neither was present here.[70]

Thus, under the law, even in a public forum, a substantial number of Supreme Court justices are concerned that explicitly religious displays visible to the public could be seen as improperly linking church and state. And more important, the law leaves states free to decline to create limited public forums in which unattended displays are visible to passersby.

In fact, of course, most local governments have not allowed anyone who so desires to erect a large display on the lawn of city hall or on the courthouse steps. Free speech for all is a vital part of American law and culture, but it does not typically extend to providing prominent government property for these purposes. Governments are concerned that minority religions, including some which are quite unpopular, would start putting their symbols in front of government buildings. They are also concerned with nonreligious speech by fringe political groups. The First Amendment, after all, extends to hateful speech, and few towns want to be associated with that.[71]

The very Supreme Court decision concerning Capitol Square in Columbus, Ohio, illustrates this problem. The cross that the Court allowed to be erected was not put up by a mainstream Christian group. The history of the controversy is, in fact, quite different.[72] In November 1993, the state of Ohio decided to allow an unattended Christmas tree in the public forum despite concerns that it might be too closely associated with the state. A few weeks later, the state granted a rabbi's application to erect a Chanukah menorah. Only then did the "Grand Titan of the Knights of the Ku Klux Klan for the Realm of Ohio" apply to erect the cross because "the Jews" were placing a "symbol of the Jewish belief" in the square.[73]

As we have seen, the Court allowed the Klan to erect its cross. In that case, Justice Thomas agreed with the Court's majority that allowing the cross did not constitute an establishment of religion, but he pointed out that the case was not really about religion:

The erection of [this] cross is a political act, not a Christian one.

There is little doubt that the Klan's main objective is to establish a racist white government in the United States. In Klan ceremony, the cross is a symbol of white supremacy and a tool for the intimidation and harassment of racial minorities, Catholics, Jews, Communists, and any other groups hated by the Klan. The cross is associated with the Klan not because of religious worship, but because of the Klan's practice of cross burning.[74]

So it is not surprising that relatively few state and local governments have decided to create limited public forums that would allow the full range of political and religious displays on public property. The Ku Klux Klan is not the only unpopular group that would assert its First Amendment rights. Governments can avoid this particular problem by erecting their own holiday displays, but then, as we have seen, the Establishment Clause requires that those displays be sapped of real religious content. Christmas trees are coupled with menorahs and signs saluting liberty, while Frosty the Snowman stands guard over crèches.

THE TRANSFORMATION OF CHANUKAH
AND THE MENORAH

There are real costs to religion in the watered-down versions of faith that appear in our public sphere. The problem gets worse when the legal doctrines intersect with the way religion is shaped by American consumerism. Let us begin with the current fate of Chanukah and the menorah before turning to the commercialization of Christmas that we have seen in the last few years.

Here is the outline of the story of Chanukah as it is known to most Jewish children in America today.[75] About 175 BC, the Jewish people were attacked by a Syrian despot who looted and desecrated the Temple in Jerusalem and forbade the Jews from practicing their religion. The Jews successfully revolted under the leadership of Judah Maccabee and liberated the Temple. While restoring the Temple, they sought to relight the eternal flame that burned there. There was only enough oil to burn for one day, yet it miraculously burned for eight days, just enough time to obtain a new supply of oil. Chanukah celebrates the victory of the Maccabees and the miracle of the oil.

Chanukah is typically celebrated in America today by virtually all Jewish families. The celebration lasts eight days and nights. Presents are given, particularly to the children. In many families, a child gets a present every night for the entire holiday. The central ritual is the lighting of the Chanukah menorah. On the first night, this nine-branched candelabra has just two candles in it. One, called the shamas, is used to light the other. On the second night, the shamas is used to light two other candles, and so on until the eighth night when all the candles are lit. The menorah represents the miracle of the oil, and brief prayers are said when it is lit each night. In addition, families play a game of chance with a spinning top called a dreidel and eat foods fried or baked in oil, such as potato pancakes.

There is nothing fundamentally mistaken in the story or the celebration I have just described. But when we look just a little deeper, we will see that the emphasis has changed so dramatically that Chanukah today is sending the opposite message from the one it sent throughout much of Jewish history. We begin with the undeniable fact that in the Jewish tradition, Chanukah is a minor holiday.[76] All normal work is permitted, and the ritual observances are minor. It stands nowhere near the High Holy Days or Passover or Shavuot or Sukkot in the Jewish calendar. It was not traditionally marked by gift giving.[77] There was a custom of giving Chanukah gelt—money—to the poor and of using some coins in games of chance, but that was it.[78]

Every observer, whether Jewish or not, recognizes that the orgies of gift giving that accompany Chanukah in America today stem solely from a coincidence of the calendar.[79] The dates of Chanukah are determined by the Hebrew calendar, which is lunar. Chanukah begins on the twenty-fifth day of Kislev, which typically falls somewhere in December.[80] As a result, the eight days of Chanukah sometimes overlap with Christmas. Because Chanukah is the Jewish holiday closest to Christmas, gift giving began so that Jewish children would not feel left out when their Christian friends received their Christmas bounty.[81] And Chanukah symbols, such as the nine-branched menorah, became prominent to offset the profusion of Christmas trees and Santa Clauses that are so prevalent in December.[82]

This sort of cultural spillover from a dominant group to a smaller one is hardly unusual. More striking is what we see when we take a closer look at the origins of Chanukah. The story most Jewish children hear today is not wrong, but it leaves out some important elements. It is true that Antiochus IV, the Seleucid king of Syria, was imposing a foreign culture on the small state of Israel or Judea around 175 BC. The culture was Greek, and Antiochus definitely wanted the Jews to adopt the Greek religion and the Greek way of learning and living. It is also true that many Jews wanted to adopt Greek ways. They wanted to assimilate, as many Jews have wanted to throughout Jewish history. The Maccabees were rebelling not just against an outside ruler but against many of their countrymen, including some important Jewish leaders.[83] Their successful rebellion was on behalf of traditional Judaism. To celebrate the Maccabees' triumph by imitating Christmas is breathtaking. A holiday that began as a protest against assimilation has become a triumph of assimilation.

The story gets even more amazing when we look more closely at the nine-branched Chanukah menorah that stands next to the Christmas tree in so many shopping centers and (when surrounded by suitable guardians such as snowmen and sleds) in public places as well. To get an idea of the role of the menorah, we have to go back to the original story of Chanukah. What is our source for the account of the revolt against Antiochus, the reclaiming of the Temple, and so on?

Chanukah does not appear in the Jewish Bible (the Old Testament), nor does it appear in the New Testament used by Protestants.[84] It is presented in the two books of the Maccabees, which are part of the Apocrypha, a set of books included in the Catholic Bible.[85] Maccabees 1 and 2 are regarded by Jews as part of our religious and historical tradition, although they hardly have the status of the Torah, the first five books of the Bible.[86]

So what do Maccabees 1 and 2 say about the miracle of the oil lasting eight days and about the Chanukah menorah? The answer is nothing.[87] Other early writers also say nothing about this. Chanukah is about the rededication of the Temple, not an eight-day miracle.[88] Indeed, some scholars believe Chanukah is celebrated for eight days because when the Maccabees took over the Temple, they celebrated Sukkot, an eight-day holiday, which they had been unable to celebrate during their military campaign.[89]

About six hundred years after the Maccabees rededicated the Temple, Chanukah was discussed in the Talmud, a vital compendium of Jewish learning.[90] Here the story of the eight-day miracle appears, as well as instructions to kindle lights in commemoration thereof. The Talmud reports that one sage called for kindling eight lights on the first day and diminishing by one each subsequent day, whereas another recommended what became the dominant custom of starting with one and adding a light each day. Jews soon began using a nine-branched Chanukah menorah to celebrate the holiday.[91]

There is nothing wrong with using the nine-branched Chanukah menorah. What is remarkable is that to many American Jews, the Chanukah menorah is synonymous with the word *menorah*. This is even more true for non-Jewish Americans, who see the Chanukah menorah in December and regard it as a central Jewish symbol. In the Torah, the menorah that God commands the Jews to build, which the Maccabees relit in the Temple, which has served as a symbol of Judaism for thousands of years, and which appears today on the emblem of the state of Israel, is not a Chanukah menorah. It has seven branches and nothing to do with gift giving. Let us look for just a moment at the story of this ancient seven-branched menorah.[92]

In the Book of Exodus, after God has led the Jewish people out of Egypt and has given them the Ten Commandments on Mount Sinai, he commands them to build a tabernacle, a portable shrine, in which several holy objects are to be kept as they travel through the desert. In particular, he commands them to build a menorah "of pure gold" (25:31) that is to weigh "a talent" (37:23–24), about seventy-five pounds. This menorah has three branches on either side of a central shaft (25:31–40).

By Jewish teachings, biblical and otherwise, this menorah went from the tabernacle into the Temple built by King Solomon in Jerusalem. That Temple was destroyed in 586 BC, but when it was rebuilt, the second Temple also had a seven-branched menorah. This is the Temple that the Maccabees rededicated. The presence of a seven-branched menorah in the second Temple is attested to by secular as well as religious sources. This Temple was refurbished by Herod beginning around 20 BC and is sometimes called Herod's Temple.[93] This is the Temple Jesus visited.[94] The historian Josephus says that the menorah in Herod's temple was "made of gold . . . a wrought lamp being attached to the extremity of each branch; of these there were seven."[95]

The second Temple was destroyed and the Jewish kingdom ended by Roman armies under the command of Titus in AD 70.[96] Shortly after Titus died, the Arch of Titus was constructed to commemorate his capture of Jerusalem.[97] This triumphal arch still stands to the southeast of the Forum in Rome, where it is visited by thousands of tourists every year.[98] One of the panels on the Arch clearly shows Roman soldiers carrying off a seven-branched menorah among other spoils of war after the destruction of Herod's Temple.[99]

Jewish law and tradition forbade making a new seven-branched menorah after the second Temple was destroyed.[100] But Jews used images of this menorah as a symbol of our faith around the world. On synagogue walls, gravestones, and jewelry, in book illustrations and elsewhere, this menorah was the primary symbol for Judaism for centuries. Only after the Renaissance did the six-pointed Star of David emerge as a better-known symbol for the religion.[101] But to this day, as its presence on the emblem of the state of Israel shows, the seven-branched menorah remains an important symbol for Judaism.[102] The emblem still appears in many synagogues and Jewish cemeteries in the United States.

If you doubt that the Chanukah menorah has overshadowed the Temple menorah, just show a picture of the latter to a Jewish child and ask what it is. Most will identify it with Chanukah, but the more attentive will ask why it has only seven branches. So the minor holiday of Chanukah, because of its proximity to Christmas, has become a gift-giving extravaganza, has lost its anti-assimilation theme, and has elevated a new symbol for Judaism—the nine-branched menorah—to prominence.

It is fair to ask if there is any real harm in this. To be sure, the fate of Chanukah is only a small part of the story about the assimilation of Judaism into American culture. And that story is not over. Judaism in all of its forms may still emerge stronger than ever in America. Thus far, however, I believe the transformation of Chanukah has not been a desirable development for American Jews.

In the writings of novelist Herman Wouk, we have eloquent testimony about how and why Chanukah has changed. He lived through this transformation and came out optimistic. Although I find his perspective invaluable, I do not share his optimism. Herman Wouk was born in New York City in 1915 to Russian immigrant parents.[103] He was raised and remained an Orthodox Jew.[104] Best known as the author of such novels as *The Caine Mutiny*, *Marjorie Morningstar*, and *The Winds of War*, he also wrote, in 1959, *This Is My God*, a well-received introduction to Orthodox Judaism.

When Wouk was a child living among Orthodox Jews in New York, he experienced what he called "the old Hanuka," a minor event not yet reshaped by Christmas:

It hardly seemed a holiday at all. Fathers left for business in the morning in work clothes. Children trudged off to school by day and scrawled homework at night. There was no celebration in the synagogue, no scroll to read, no colorful customs, no Bible story. For eight nights running, one's father . . . chanted a melody heard only at this time . . . and . . . lit candles.[105]

By 1959, Wouk was aware that Judaism had "a new Hanuka": "By a total accident of timing, this minor Hebrew celebration falls close in the calendar year to a great holy day of the Christian faith."[106] And what happened to that old holiday? "The colossal jamboree of the department-store Christmas of course overwhelmed it like a tidal wave."[107] Every Jewish kid wanted to celebrate Chanukah, at least to the extent of getting gifts. As I have said, Wouk saw a bright side here:

If the old custom of Hanuka money has become the new custom of Hanuka gifts, that is a minor shift in manners. The tale of the Feast of Lights, with its all-too-sharp comment on our life nowadays, is very colorful. It is of the greatest use in giving the young a quick grasp of the Jewish historic situation. The gifts win their attention. The little candles stimulate their questions. The observance seems tooled to the needs of self-discovery.[108]

My own sense is that in the many years since Wouk wrote that assessment, Chanukah has not had the positive impact he foresaw. In terms of total numbers, at least, people have been drifting away from Judaism. Many large factors are at work, of course, in the fact that the Jewish population in the United States today is no larger than it was in 1959, remarkable when you consider that half a million Jews have immigrated during that time period and the nation's population as a whole has grown dramatically.[109] If putting the menorah next to the Christmas tree provided an "all-too-sharp comment on our life nowadays," I am afraid it is not the anti-assimilation comment Herman Wouk (and Judah Maccabee) had in mind.

MOVING CHRISTMAS TO THE
HEART OF THE ECONOMY

Unlike Chanukah, Christmas is obviously a major religious holiday. For centuries, Christians around the world have celebrated the birth of the Savior, often in church services. Because the Gospels do not state the date or even the season of Jesus' birth, the timing of the holiday was not fixed by the early Christians.[110] Clement, a bishop of Alexandria, put Jesus' birthday at November 18, whereas others, arguing that the shepherds described in the Gospels were in the fields, chose dates in the spring or summer.[111] In the fourth century after Jesus' birth, church leaders fixed the celebration at December 25, in part to compete with and incorporate the pagan celebration of Saturnalia, which took place around the winter solstice.[112]

As Christmas celebrations spread through Europe over the centuries, various winter symbols became part of Christmas. Evergreen trees that played a symbolic role in northern European culture became Christmas trees.[113] St. Nicholas, whose name day fell in the winter, became associated with Christmas as well.[114]

In early America, Christmas observances varied. The Southern Atlantic colonies followed English customs, such as drinking from the wassail bowl.[115] In New York and Pennsylvania, northern European practices, including the Christmas tree, became prevalent.[116] In Puritan New England, Christmas celebrations were repressed, even made illegal for a time, because of their association with pagan rituals and rowdy public displays such as excessive drinking.[117]

By the middle of the nineteenth century, Americans were celebrating Christmas with a combination of religious services and family traditions that are similar to those prevalent today.[118] In particular, the giving of gifts, particularly to children, became extraordinarily important. The Christmas tree evolved into a place where the gifts were put, while Santa Claus, through the poetry of Clement Moore, the cartoons of Thomas Nast, and the commercials of the Coca-Cola Company, became the genial dispenser of gifts from the North Pole.[119] For almost two hundred years, Christians have lived with the tension between the emphasis on gifts and the sacred message of Jesus' birth. It is a difficult struggle in a culture where the *Wall Street Journal* devotes more coverage to Christmas than do many church publications, since the entire economy suffers if Christmas sales are weak.

But commercialism has never fully obliterated Christmas, and Christians have long seen the downside of too much gift giving. In 1834, a religious magazine in Boston printed the views of a reader who was "amazed at the cunning skill with which the most worthless as well as most valuable articles are set forth to tempt and decoy the bewildered purchaser."[120] Harriet Beecher Stowe wrote a story in 1850 in which a character bemoaned the loss of those Christmases past when "presents did not fly about as they do now. . . . There are worlds of money wasted, at this time of year, in getting things that nobody wants, and nobody cares for after they are got."[121]

By 1894, an editorial in the *New York Tribune* directly criticized the materialism of the season: "As soon as the Thanksgiving turkey is eaten, the great question of buying Christmas presents begins to take the terrifying shape it has come to assume in recent years. . . . The season of Christmas needs to be dematerialized."[122] In 1909, *Lippincott's Magazine* printed an article that was happy to report a backlash against the increasing commercialization of Christmas:

That Yuletide has come to be anticipated—with trepidation—is no secret. Each year this becomes more obvious. With midwinter comes the nerve-wrecking realization that before many days all good "Christians" must be prepared somehow to spend money that they cannot afford, to purchase "things" the recipients do not want. . . . Happily, there is a growing revolt against this state of affairs.[123]

Throughout the twentieth century, the back and forth between the commercial and the religious continued. In 1998, for example, Bill McKibben published a book promoting the Hundred Dollar Holiday program he and some friends started in which they tried to limit the amount of money they spent on Christmas to one hundred dollars:

We were Christians, and we felt that the story of the birth of this small baby who would become our Savior, a story that should be full of giddy joy, could hardly break through to our hearts amid all the rush and fuss of the season. And many of our friends, Christian or not, felt that too much of the chance for family togetherness was being robbed by the pressures of Christmas busyness and the tensions of gift-giving.[124]

But in the early years of the twenty-first century a new voice was heard. Some Christian spokespeople, astonishing as it seems, urged that Christmas be moved further into the marketplace. My focus in this book is on the cost to religion when it is forced into the public square. Because of our constitutional traditions and the diversity of our culture, a purely religious symbol, such as the crèche, will suffer in the public square, where it has to be surrounded by secular symbols. Its meaning and impact will inevitably be diluted and distorted.

A premise of my view is that true religion can be freely expressed in the private sphere, including homes and churches, and that this is central to the preservation of the real religious values so vital to millions of Americans. From my point of view—and this is not a matter of controversy—there is no legal problem with religious symbols being displayed in private stores and shopping malls. Of course, merchants are seeking to make money, so they will typically display those icons—such as Santa Claus—that are associated with spending.

Until a few years ago, it never had occurred to me that religious spokespeople would urge that Santa Claus and slogans like "Merry Christmas" be given *more* prominence in the American marketplace. First of all, they are fairly prominent as it is. More important, for over a hundred years Christians have suggested that a little less, rather than a little more, commercialism might be a good thing for Christmas. So when I question the movement to make salespeople greet their customers with a hearty "Merry Christmas," I am certainly not making a legal argument. But I cannot help noting that this movement has the same effect as surrounding a crèche with Santa Claus and a Christmas tree—it is hollowing out religion and making it ever harder to find a faith that transcends our day-to-day desires.

John Gibson's 2005 book, *The War on Christmas*, begins with the story of a father of a student at a private school who is distressed that the school displayed a "friendship tree" because the principal did not want to "offend people" by calling it a Christmas tree.[125] The father is unhappy because, as he puts it, "I want my son to know what a Christmas tree is."[126] Upon hearing that the father might remove his son from the school, the friendship tree became a Christmas tree.[127]

At first I did not understand the point of the story. Of course, private schools can display Christmas trees and call them Christmas trees, as this school ultimately did. Indeed, there are pervasively religious private schools that have actual religious icons and real religious services, not just Christmas trees. If a father feels his son needs to learn in school "what a Christmas tree is," it is not hard to find a school that will help, as the school in Gibson's anecdote eventually did.

I did not catch on until I turned a few pages in *The War on Christmas* and saw the author reprint with approval a letter to the *Times* in London:

As many as 80,000 Brits . . . live in the United Arab Emirates, where the country's indigenous people live by Sharia (Islamic law). Yet shopping centres are decorated with Christmas finery, stores pipe Christmas tunes to every corner, malls are full of children of all nationalities excitedly queuing to see Santa. . . .

Hotels hold tree-lighting ceremonies and carol services by swimming pools, and holidaymakers stand amazed when Santa rides into town on a camel, handing out gifts.

I have heard of no local being offended by any of these supposed insults and no one complains of being singled out for persecution.[128]

Then I understood. The author of the letter and the author of the book wanted more Santa Clauses and Christmas trees throughout America.

The War on Christmas was motivated by the same concerns that drove other Christians at about the same time to decry commercial establishments that were not putting enough emphasis on Christmas. At one point in 2005, a Catholic advocacy group briefly launched a boycott against Wal-Mart for failing to consistently use "Merry Christmas" instead of "Happy Holidays" in its merchandising.[129] The American Family Association called for a boycott of Target stores on similar grounds. The president of the association said he wanted to see Target use "Merry Christmas" signs throughout their stores, "if they expect Christians to come in and buy products during this so-called season."[130]

Americans have a right to speak out against sales practices they find offensive and to take their business where they please, and stores have a right to attract customers. I think it is safe to say that most merchants in America will do what they can to encourage "Christians to come in and buy products." Indeed, in November 2006, Wal-Mart, "[w]ishing for a bigger holiday season after a sluggish fall," announced that more of its merchandise would be labeled "Christmas" than in the previous year.[131] The transformation of a sacred holiday into a marketing slogan continues to gather speed. I suppose I should not be surprised to find that some Christians view buying products while standing under Merry Christmas signs to be the essence of Christmas. I believe that a misguided effort to force religion into the public square waters down faith, and this is a related example of a similar phenomenon.

Let me return for a moment to that letter about Santa Claus in the United Arab Emirates. The constitution of that nation declares that Islam is the official religion of the state.[132] The government of the United Arab Emirates prohibits Christians and other non-Muslims from proselytizing or distributing religious literature under penalty of criminal prosecution and imprisonment.[133] The presence of Santa Claus and the Christmas tree in the United Arab Emirates does not establish that the nation accepts Christianity. It establishes that, to them, Santa Claus and the Christmas tree have nothing to do with Christianity. The same point could be made around the globe. In parts of China, Christians have to worship in secret for fear of persecution, while nearby shops feature Christmas trees and workers dressed as Santa's helpers.[134]

In America, Christians can worship without fear of persecution. The real threat is being swallowed up by secular, commercial forces that Christians in America have resisted for centuries. Religion loses its distinctive meaning when it must be distorted and diminished in order to appear on a courthouse lawn in a diverse society. It also loses its soul when it is thrust ever more deeply into the world of sales and profits.

CHAPTER 5

Neither France nor Iran:
Religious Freedom in America

THE DISPUTES OVER POSTING the Ten Commandments in court-houses, teaching intelligent design in public schools, and putting crèches in front of city hall are exhausting for everyone involved. They diminish religion while leaving angry believers and nonbelievers in their wake. Fortunately, these disputes tell us very little about religious freedom in America. Indeed, they mislead us.

According to many of those who try to force religion into county courthouses, America is a godless nation. Yet we are, in fact, one of the most religious nations on earth. In America, Christianity has avoided the collapse it has suffered in Western Europe. At the same time, other faiths flourish here as well. Analyzing the reasons for the success of religion in America will enable us to look away from the morass that characterizes religion in the public square to the more important pro-tections for faith that we must preserve.

We will begin by looking at the cultural and legal basis for religious freedom in America. We will then show why a forced marriage of church and state is good for neither.

NEITHER FRANCE NOR IRAN

Every Christmas, the government of Paris uses the taxpayers' money to put up hundreds of Christmas trees, decorated with lights, on the Champs-Elysées.[1] But this sort of display cannot hide the decline of reli-gion in France. As with much of Western Europe, churchgoing, religious affiliation, and belief in God are on the decline throughout France.[2] On paper, religion in France ought to be much like religion in the United States. Both nations are predominantly Christian, but with a strong rep-resentation of Jewish, Muslim, and other faiths.[3] Both nations observe a legal separation of church and state in most respects. France is known for a particularly strong belief in secular government, although it is worth noting that the French directly fund private religious schools and pay for the upkeep of some churches.[4]

But in terms of the religious beliefs of its citizens, the United States is in many respects more like Iran, where church and state are not separated, than it is like France. When survey takers asked citizens in the three nations if they believed in God, 99 percent in Iran and 94 percent in the United States said "yes"; only 56 percent gave that answer in France.[5] Similarly, in France, 60 percent of those surveyed say they "never" attend religious services, an answer given by only 4 percent in Iran and 14 percent in the United States.[6] Perhaps most dramatic, when asked, "Independently of whether you go to church or not, would you say you are 'a religious person,'" 82 percent of those surveyed in the United States and Iran said "yes," whereas only 44 percent in France gave that answer.[7]

Yet the religious makeup and legal situation in Iran are fundamentally different from those in the United States and France. Muslims make up over 99 percent of the Iranian population, and, unlike in the United States and France, minority religions are not allowed to worship in peace.[8] Moreover, under Iranian law, Islam is the official religion of the state, and all laws and regulations must be consistent with Islamic law.[9]

The United States has a combination of a deeply religious citizenry and freedom for religious minorities that is found in neither France nor Iran. This is not a matter of chance, nor is it an unfathomable mystery. Our cultural and legal traditions very clearly reject both a secular and a theocratic society. These traditions are well worth keeping.

A simple example demonstrates how differently religious exercise is treated in the United States than elsewhere. Consider a young Muslim woman who is attending public school. Can she choose whether to wear the head scarf that some Muslims believe their religion requires? In Iran she has no choice. She must wear the head scarf; indeed, women must be dressed according to conservative Islamic teachings whenever they appear in public.[10] She also has no choice in France. Pursuant to a 2004 law, public school students cannot wear any apparel that conspicuously shows their religious affiliation.[11] Jewish students cannot wear skullcaps, Christian students cannot wear large crosses, and Muslim students cannot wear head scarves. The law was clearly aimed at the growing number of Muslim women who had begun wearing head scarves in school.[12] In the United States, the student has a choice. The government cannot make her wear a head scarf or forbid it.[13] In reality, many students in American public schools choose to wear visible religious apparel, and many others do not. This result, strongly favored by liberals, moderates, and conservatives across the country, symbolizes the role of religion and religious freedom in the United States today.

THE LIMITED ROLE FOR GOVERNMENT EXPRESSIONS OF FAITH

How did this relationship between government and religion develop in the United States? It begins with the Constitution and with the American approach of treating the public and private spheres quite differently. The First Amendment to the United States Constitution begins, "Congress shall make no law respecting an establishment of religion, or prohibiting the free exercise thereof." The Fourteenth Amendment has been interpreted to apply the same standard to the states.[14] Legal disputes over religion in the public square implicate the first part of this amendment, the Establishment Clause. When you put that together with the second part, the Free Exercise Clause, as well as with the constitutional protection for free speech, you can see why our law draws such a sharp distinction between public and private behavior.

If the federal government were to put large, permanent crosses on every door and in every room of its buildings, the government would be tilting the balance in favor of Christianity so greatly that the Supreme Court would find an unconstitutional establishment of religion because the government itself would be sending a message with those crosses. If all Christians in America put a large, permanent cross on every door and in every room of their houses, there would be no establishment of religion. All citizens have a right to display religious symbols on their private property under free exercise and free speech principles.

The law, therefore, does not forbid the display of religious symbols—it limits the government's use of those symbols. For this reason, the government is driven, when it tries to support religion, to shape its activities so that they appear secular or to argue that it is merely recognizing religion as a historical fact rather than as a force that changes people's lives. The historical argument is obviously not frivolous, and there is no reason that it has to be ignored. Recognizing a historical pattern is not the same as actually following religious teachings; indeed, there are times when it is a sensible thing to do. In fact, many American leaders, from the earliest days of the country to the present, have drawn strength from their belief in God and have believed that America draws strength from God's protection. Not every prominent American shares this view, and the Constitution itself does not mention God, but it would be a misreading of history to ignore this part of the American story.

IN GOD WE TRUST

Since the founding of this nation, many recognitions of God have become evident in the American landscape. Perhaps the best known is the appearance of "In God We Trust" on our coins and currency. This phrase was not put in place by the framers of the Constitution. When Congress approved the Great Seal of the United States in 1782, it included, as it does now, the Latin phrase *E Pluribus Unum*, "Out of Many, One."[15] During the Civil War, Congress authorized placing "In God We Trust" on some currency.[16] Its use eventually spread to our money generally.[17] In 1956, in part to distinguish the United States from the formally atheistic Soviet Union, Congress passed a law making "In God We Trust" the national motto.[18]

When court challenges have been brought against the use of "In God We Trust" on our currency and elsewhere, judges have uniformly rejected them on the ground that the phrase is not an endorsement of religion but as a recognition of our history and, at most, a kind of "ceremonial deism" that does not entangle church and state.[19] Obviously not everyone agrees—some observers, such as Theodore Roosevelt, have felt that putting God on the currency cheapens religion and comes "dangerously close to sacrilege"[20]—but it is a settled practice today.

THE PLEDGE OF ALLEGIANCE

A somewhat more controversial dispute concerns the use of the Pledge of Allegiance in the public schools, since the pledge contains the phrase "under God." Lower courts have upheld the pledge, and in the one case in which a court did not, the Supreme Court set the decision aside.[21] The Court, however, ruled on technical grounds, so although it is quite likely the Court would uphold the pledge, the matter is worth looking at in a bit more detail.

As we have seen, the Supreme Court held in 1943 that any student can be excused from reciting the pledge because free speech principles prevent the government from forcing anyone to affirm a belief that is personally abhorrent.[22] Jehovah's Witnesses won this case on the ground that reciting the pledge made them bow down to "graven images" in violation of the Ten Commandments, but the principle applies to anyone with religious or political objections to the pledge. But in 1943, the pledge did not include "under God." Moreover, in cases beginning in the 1960s, the Court struck down prayer in the public schools, even though some schools allowed students to be excused when the prayers were said.[23] The Court believes that beginning the school day with a prayer sends a message of government support for religion that is unacceptable even if students can be excused. Moreover, the Court has expressed concern that peer pressure might coerce students into saying prayers they find offensive despite their theoretical right to be excused.[24] So from time to time, lawsuits are brought stating that a student's undoubted ability to be excused from the pledge is not enough. Since the pledge now says that we are a nation "under God," there is an unconstitutional establishment of religion when the pledge is recited in the public schools. But is the

Pledge of Allegiance a prayer or a religious observance at all? It is likely that the Supreme Court believes not. Some history is helpful here.

The pledge, as originally written by a private citizen in 1892, read "I pledge allegiance to my Flag and to the Republic for which it stands, one nation, indivisible, with liberty and justice for all."[25] In the early 1920s, the National Flag Conference changed "my Flag" to "the Flag of the United States of America."[26] In 1942, Congress formalized this version as part of an effort to "codify and emphasize existing rules and customs pertaining to the display and use of the flag."[27] Local school boards had the authority to decide whether to begin the school day with the pledge. Many of them did, and, as noted, in 1943 the Supreme Court ruled that students had a right to be excused from reciting it.

The matter of religion entered the story in 1954 when Congress amended the pledge to include the words "under God," so today it reads: "I pledge Allegiance to the Flag of the United States of America, and to the Republic for which it stands, one Nation under God, indivisible, with liberty and justice for all."[28] The sponsor of the 1954 amendment, Representative Rabout, said his goal was to contrast the American belief in God with the Soviet Union's embrace of atheism.[29] However one characterizes America's attitude toward religion, it is surely correct that we reject the Soviet oppression of religious expression. Thus, the motivation behind "under God" in the pledge was similar to that which led Congress in 1956 to denominate "In God We Trust" as the national motto. We were drawing a contrast between ourselves and the Soviet Union.

When the question of whether "under God" in the pledge constituted an unconstitutional establishment of religion came before the Supreme Court in 2004, a majority of the Court declined to resolve the dispute on the ground that the parent bringing the case lacked legal custody of the child whose views he sought to represent.[30] However, those justices who did reach the merits of the case all agreed that the pledge was constitutional. Chief Justice Rehnquist, joined by Justice O'Connor, found that the pledge "is a patriotic observance. . . . [T]he phrase 'under God' is in no sense a prayer, nor an endorsement of any religion."[31] It simply reflects, Rehnquist and O'Connor argued, the historical role religion has played in our nation's history. Justice Thomas agreed that the pledge was constitutional.[32] Even the majority opinion by Justice Stevens, in the course of declining to resolve the matter, described the pledge as "a common public acknowledgment of the ideals that our flag symbolizes. Its recitation is a patriotic exercise designed to foster national unity and pride in those principles."[33]

So it is unlikely that the Court views the pledge as unconstitutional. However one feels about that issue, it is, like the Christmas tree in the town square, largely a symbolic matter. This sort of dispute over the use of the word *God* is a side show with little relevance to how most Americans practice their religion.

For politicians, it is certainly helpful to invoke "God," but for most people of faith their religion has more specific teachings. When political leaders start to talk about religion, they often aim for the lowest common denominator in order to gain wide support. As President Eisenhower has been quoted as saying, "Our government makes no sense unless it is founded in a deeply felt religious faith—and I don't care what it is."[34]

THE ROBUST ROLE FOR
PRIVATE RELIGIOUS EXPRESSION

Millions of Americans do care what their faith says. Fortunately for private citizens, if not for government bureaucracies, real religious freedom exists in America. It exists because of several provisions in our Constitution and laws. First of all, the First Amendment protection of free speech applies to religious speech. We have already seen a narrow implication of this: the government cannot discriminate against religious viewpoints when it creates a limited public forum, a kind of mini–Hyde Park Speakers' Corner. If the state allows the after-hours use of public school classrooms for political and ethical discussions, it has to allow religious discussions as well.

But the First Amendment protection for religious speech has even broader implications for religion. Because of free speech, when you talk to your neighbor, you can talk openly about your view of God, something that history teaches we should never take for granted. And politicians do not surrender this right. They, too, can invoke God in their speeches, and they often do. More generally, the First Amendment's protection of freedom of association means you can band together in communities of faith, without having to admit nonbelievers to your services and meetings.[35]

Religious beliefs can shape your political beliefs. The civil rights movement led by the Reverend Martin Luther King, and the right to life movement, which has many prominent ministers among its leaders, are examples of mass movements in which many participants are motivated by their faith.[36] Any laws that result have to have secular as well as religious bases, but that does not negate the reasons people get involved.[37]

Free speech also means you can, as a private citizen, try to win converts to your faith. Just as the government cannot forbid you from preaching Marxism, it cannot forbid you from proselytizing for Christianity, or for any other religion. It does not matter whether you are preaching the most popular or the most obscure faith.

THE CONSTITUTIONAL RIGHT
TO USE PRIVATE SCHOOLS

Free speech is only the beginning of the constitutional protections for real religious exercise. Less well known, but extraordinarily important, is the fact that the United States Supreme Court has interpreted the Constitution's due process clause to protect every adult's right to send his or her child to private school, including religious school.[38] Thus, neither the state nor the federal government can force you to use the public schools, something a few states tried to do in the 1920s.[39] This right extends to home schooling as well.[40] The government can set minimum standards for what must be conveyed in school, but the actual curriculum in private and home school settings is often very different from what it is in the public schools.[41] In particular, religious instruction is quite common.[42]

In practice, this is an enormous protection for religion in America.

More than a million Americans every year send their children to private schools, and the vast majority of those are religious schools, where the explicit teaching of religious faith and ethics—indeed, where formal worship services—are often part of the school program.[43] For parents who want a pervasively religious environment for their children, this constitutional right is of central importance. Private schools can be central to the transmission of religious values through the generations.

Of course, private schools cost money, and not everyone can afford them. But the Supreme Court has also held that the government, if it wishes to pick up the tab, can provide parents with vouchers that can be used to pay tuition at any private school, including religious schools.[44] This 2002 voucher decision was controversial, but the majority reached its conclusion by using a version of the public-private distinction we have seen before. When the government gives you money, and you choose how to spend that money, that spending decision is yours. You can use unemployment benefits to buy a Bible without anyone saying that the government is buying Bibles, so you can use vouchers for a religious school on the same principle.

The dissenting justices in the 2002 voucher case believed the program was too closely linked to predictable benefits to religious schools, but the majority believed this concern was not relevant because parents, not the government, were deciding whether to spend their money on religious or nonreligious schools.[45]

My own view is that religious schools want to be careful before agreeing to become involved with voucher programs because with government money often comes government control. However, if the taxpayers want to fund vouchers and schools choose to accept them, private religious schools will appeal to even more parents.

THE ESSENCE OF FREE EXERCISE

Finally, there is the explicit constitutional protection for the free exercise of religion. On two very basic points concerning this part of the First Amendment, the United States Supreme Court has been completely consistent and clear. First, the government cannot question or punish your religious beliefs. There can be no heresy trials in America.

This issue came before the Supreme Court in 1944 when it considered whether a jury in a fraud case could consider whether the religious views of the defendant were factually true.[46] Although the Court held that a defendant who is trying to sell you something with a religious pitch could be liable if he knowingly lied to you, the truth or falsity of his underlying faith was off limits.[47] As Justice Douglas wrote:

Heresy trials are foreign to our Constitution. Men may believe what they cannot prove. . . . Religious experiences which are as real as life to some may be incomprehensible to others. . . . Many take their gospel from the New Testament. But it would hardly be supposed that they could be tried before a jury charged with the duty of determining whether those teachings contained false representations. The miracles of the New Testament, the Divinity of Christ, life after death, the power of prayer are deep in the religious convictions of many. If one could be sent to jail because a jury in a hostile environment found those teachings false, little indeed would be left of religious freedom.[48]

The second area of clear agreement goes beyond your beliefs to the way you exercise them, that is, to the rituals and practices of your faith. The Court has consistently held that the government cannot burden the exercise of your religion because it thinks your religion is not the true faith. For example, in 1993 the Supreme Court stopped a Florida town from banning the sacrifice of chickens, a ritual practiced there by the Santerian faith. The town had continued to allow the killing of chickens and other animals for all other purposes; they were simply trying to ban a religious practice they found offensive, and the Court unanimously said they could not do so.[49]

These two principles, important as they are, leave a major problem concerning free exercise unresolved. What if the government wants to ban a practice for genuine public policy reasons, but it turns out this practice is an important religious ritual for some of its citizens? For example, what if a religion uses a dangerous drug in its sacraments or practices snake handling? What if a town, for public health reasons, wants to ban the killing of all animals within its city limits, and this has the incidental effect of preventing the Santerians from performing an important ritual? This problem does not have an easy answer. No court has ever maintained that freedom of religious exercise is absolute. It is too easy to imagine a religion that practices human sacrifice. So where do we draw the line?

The Supreme Court today approaches the matter as follows. A genuinely neutral law, not aimed at a religious practice, will be upheld even if it has the incidental effect of burdening that practice. Thus, for example, the Court held in 1990 that a ban on the use of the hallucinogenic drug peyote can be applied to Native Americans, even though the use of peyote is a central sacrament in their faith.[50] But there are two important caveats. First, the legislature can exempt Native Americans from this ban without exempting nonreligious users.[51] In fact, both the federal government and many state governments have passed statutes allowing Native Americans to use peyote in their rituals.[52] Second, the legislature can, if it chooses, enact a statute allowing religious practices generally to be excused from any law that burdens them unless the government can show a compelling interest in imposing the law on the practice. Under this kind of general statute, the courts have to decide in each case whether the government has met its burden of showing a compelling state interest.

The federal government has passed just such a general law. It is called the Religious Freedom Restoration Act,[53] and the Supreme Court has upheld it as it applies to the federal government's own behavior. As a result, whenever a federal law burdens a religious practice, the religious group can go to court. They will be allowed to continue their practice unless the federal government can show that it has a compelling state interest in stopping the religious exercise.

In 2006, a unanimous Supreme Court applied the Religious Freedom Restoration Act to uphold the right of a small group to use a controlled substance in its sacraments.[54] The case provides a window into the state of religious freedom in America today. O Centro Espírita Beneficente União do Vegetal (UDV) is a Christian group based in Brazil with a small American branch. They receive communion through a sacramental tea called *hoasca*, which is brewed from plants unique to the Amazon region. *Hoasca* contains demethyltryptamine (DMT), a hallucinogen listed in Schedule I of the federal Controlled Substances Act.[55] In 1999, United States Customs inspectors seized a shipment of *hoasca* bound for the American UDV and threatened the church members with prosecution. A lawsuit ensued, and the case ultimately reached the Supreme Court.[56]

The battle was squarely joined in the high court. On the one hand, the Controlled Substances Act states that Schedule I substances, such as DMT, have "a high potential for abuse" and "no currently accepted medical use in treatment in the United States."[57] Moreover, no one maintained that the ban of DMT had been aimed at any religious practice. Finally, unlike the peyote situation, Congress had not passed a special statute allowing the religious use of DMT by the UDV church.

On the other hand, the government conceded that UDV's use of *hoasca* was a sincere exercise of religion rather than a sham designed to allow recreational use of a drug.[58] And, most important, the government conceded that under the Religious Freedom Restoration Act it had the burden of persuading the Court that there was a compelling interest in preventing the small UDV group from using DMT and that no less restrictive alternative would serve the government's purposes.[59] The federal government sought to meet its burden by showing that seizing *hoasca* was necessary to protect the health of UDV members, because DMT can cause psychotic reactions and cardiac irregularities, and to prevent the diversion of *hoasca* to recreational users.[60] More generally, the government argued that the Controlled Substances Act creates a "closed" system: allowing religious exceptions would lead to a request for more exceptions, and the public would mistakenly believe such exceptions mean that a drug is not really harmful.[61]

But at trial, the government had not been able to prove its case. UDV demonstrated that when used in the sacramental setting, DMT did not endanger members and that the small amount of *hoasca* imported by the church did not pose a diversion risk.[62] The unanimous Supreme Court relied on these findings, and Chief Justice Roberts, in his opinion for the Court, issued a sharp response to the government's contention that exceptions for religious groups would be unworkable:

> The Government's argument echoes the classic rejoinder of bureaucrats throughout history: If I make an exception for you, I'll have to make one for everybody, so no exceptions. But RFRA [the Religious Freedom Restoration Act] operates by mandating consideration, under the compelling interest test, of exceptions to "rule[s] of general applicability." . . . Congress determined that the legislated test "is a workable test for striking sensible balances between religious liberty and competing prior governmental interests."[63]

So, as a matter of federal law, religious exercise receives vital protection. It cannot be burdened unless the government has a compelling interest, and the courts will take that test seriously.

Many states have followed suit. Although the Supreme Court has held that the federal government lacks the power to impose the federal Religious Freedom Restoration Act on the states,[64] states are free to use this approach if they make the choice on their own. In several states, legislatures have chosen to use the federal approach: there is a requirement that no state law can burden a religious practice unless the government can convince a court of a compelling state interest in applying that law to the practice.[65]

In the other states, religious groups must rely on specific legislation exempting a particular practice from a general law. In the absence of a specific exemption, the practice will be banned unless the religion can convince the court that the law was aimed at religion or that the law violates some other constitutional provision. It may fairly be said that in these states, minority religions are at a disadvantage since they may lack the lobbying power to win exemptions from state laws when their practices violate those laws. There is evidence, however, that people of many backgrounds often band together to win religious exemptions for minority groups, as the presence of numerous state laws protecting Native American use of peyote suggests.

HARMONIZING THE ESTABLISHMENT AND FREE EXERCISE CLAUSES

The combination of non-establishment and free exercise values prevents the United States from becoming either France or Iran. The secular system in France, in which religious exemptions from the law are essentially unknown, tramples on our sense of free exercise. The Iranian theocracy, in which Islamic law governs everyone, is an obviously unacceptable establishment of religion under American law.

The trick in our system is to harmonize non-establishment and free exercise. As the Supreme Court has noted, either principle, "if expanded to a logical extreme, would tend to clash with the other."[66] If the slightest accommodation of religious observance is considered an improper establishment of religion, free exercise in America would be a hollow promise. Consider a dry county in the South in which the consumption of alcohol is forbidden. If religious exemptions were forbidden, the local sheriff would be free to imprison Catholics for using wine in communion. And if any infringement on a religion's teachings constituted an improper abridgment of free exercise, we would all be at the mercy of the most wide-reaching faiths. Imagine a religion that taught that everyone in the society, believer or not, had to bow down to the gods of its religion. If we granted that request in the name of free exercise, we would have an established religion.

Such situations explain why the Court has struggled so mightily to make its way through the religion clauses. Almost any action the government takes, even when it is trying to be neutral, can be seen as upsetting the delicate balance created by the two religion clauses. As the Supreme Court decision involving the religion that uses *hoasca* demonstrates, the law has begun to move toward accepting legislative accommodations in these cases. Indeed, accommodation has become the touchstone for much of what goes on in this area.

Accommodation can come in several forms. The Court has been receptive to both general statutes, such as those that allow a religious practice unless there is a compelling state interest on the other side, and to specific legislative exemptions, such as those that allow Native Americans to use peyote. Of course, if every statute that favored religion could be justified simply by calling it an accommodation, there would be nothing left of the Establishment Clause. The Court has said that it will test a legislative accommodation by asking if it is needed to remove an exceptional government-created burden on a private religious exercise, if it succeeds without burdening people of other faiths, and if it is available equally to all religions.[67]

The first of these factors demonstrates why the accommodation idea is not relevant when we are trying to decide whether to allow a religious display on government property or the teaching of an arguably religious doctrine in public school. In neither case has the government done anything to burden your free exercise of religion. As a result, when confronting religion in the public square, the Court has to fall back on Establishment Clause doctrines like endorsement or coercion. But the accommodation idea, although it may not appear in the news as often as the latest Christmas tree case, is far more important because it deals with the actual practice of religion in America.

Finding your way between the Establishment and Free Exercise Clauses is like walking a tightrope. But it is a walk worth taking to preserve the unique brand of religious freedom we have in the United States. The accommodation principle is not empty or banal. When you say, as the Court has, that a legislature can allow a religious group to use an otherwise illegal drug, without giving the same privilege to a secular philosopher who wants to try the drug, some will say you have favored religion too much. Indeed, some will say that you have established religion. But if you forbid all legislative accommodations, free exercise drops out of the picture.[68] In upholding the application of the Religious Freedom Restoration Act to federal laws, the Supreme Court made clear that religion can be favored over nonreligion in the accommodation setting. The Free Exercise Clause is not meaningless.

DEFINING RELIGION

Because the First Amendment singles out religion for special treatment, the courts at times have to decide if a particular set of beliefs constitutes a religion for constitutional purposes. Although defining religion can cause headaches for philosophers and theologians, it has rarely caused problems in the courts. Fortunately for all of us, the courts have taken a commonsense view of the meaning of religion. They have defined it broadly enough to reach the wide range of faiths that matter so much to so many Americans, but not so broadly as to pull in secular areas such as scientific teachings. Viewing science as religion is bad for both: science cannot tell us how to live our lives, and it proceeds by its own internal methodology.

Most of the legal work in this area has been done by lower courts. In fact, the United States Supreme Court has never squarely defined religion for First Amendment purposes. The reason is surprisingly simple: in the Free Exercise and Establishment Clause cases it has decided, no one on either side has questioned whether the group in question was religious. The cases have involved either mainstream faiths such as Christianity or Judaism; smaller Christian sects such as Jehovah's Witnesses; or less well-known but clearly religious practices such as those involving Santerians, an African-Caribbean faith that has adopted some Catholic rituals, or Native Americans who seek to protect obviously religious activities.

During the Vietnam War, the Supreme Court was called upon to construe the federal law granting conscientious objector status to those with religious objections to war.[69] But these cases involved the meaning of a statute, not the Constitution. The Court construed the statutory concept of religion broadly in these cases, finding that Congress wanted to exempt those who opposed all war on strongly held, overarching moral grounds. Congress could have forced the Court to confront the constitutional issue by amending the law to define religion more narrowly, but it did not do so. Ultimately, Congress ratified a broad statutory definition for conscientious objectors, which it clearly has the power to do.

Supreme Court justices have occasionally made nonbinding statements about the meaning of religion in cases in which the issue was not before them. In a 1972 case involving the rights of the Amish, a Christian group that shuns many aspects of modern life, Chief Justice Burger said that "if the Amish asserted their claims because of their subjective evaluation and rejection of the contemporary secular values accepted by the majority, much as Thoreau rejected the social values of his time and isolated himself at Walden Pond, their claims would not rest on a religious basis. Thoreau's choice was philosophical and personal rather than religious."[70] But the case did not require the chief justice to draw the line between the religious and the philosophical.

About a decade earlier, Justice Black made a passing reference to "Secular Humanism" that has led to some confusion and controversy. In particular, some opponents of the theory of evolution have said that teaching that theory in the schools amounts to an establishment of religion because the theory of evolution is part of the religion of secular humanism. These opponents have at times cited Black's comment for support. But this contention is both mistaken and deeply misguided. It is mistaken because Black's comment, which had no bearing on the resolution of the case before him, concerned a specific state court opinion dealing with a particular group's status under state tax law. Here is what happened.

In 1961, the Supreme Court unanimously agreed that a Maryland state constitutional provision requiring that state office holders declare their belief in God was an unconstitutional infringement on an atheist's freedom of belief.[71] In the course of his opinion, Justice Black, in a footnote, said, "Among religions in this country which do not teach what would generally be considered a belief in the existence of God are Buddhism, Taoism, . . . Secular Humanism."[72] For the assertion about "Secular Humanism," Black cited a 1957 California case in which a state court allowed a property tax exemption for a group called the Fellowship of Humanity.[73]

In the 1957 case, the California court had been called upon to apply a statute that allowed a tax exemption for property used "solely and exclusively for religious worship."[74] The court found that the group in question qualified: they used their property for weekly Sunday meetings, which included periods of meditation, the singing of Fellowship songs, and occasional Bible readings.[75] I cannot say whether the California court correctly construed their state law in that property tax case a half century ago. I can say that a state statutory decision allowing a tax exemption for a specific group that gathered for Sunday meetings in Oakland, California, does not define the meaning of religion in the United States Constitution.

Far more important, the effort to say that believing in evolution is a religion is exactly backward. It diminishes religion and elevates science to a status it does not deserve.[76] Believing in a particular scientific teaching does not tell you how to live your life, how to think about the afterlife, or how to understand the existence and nature of God. If a scientist claims otherwise, in public school or anywhere else, he or she should be challenged immediately.

On occasion, the lower courts, unlike the United States Supreme Court, have been called upon to define religion for First Amendment purposes. One of these decisions has gained wide support in the judiciary and among scholars, and thus has created the closest thing we have to a working definition of religion in constitutional law. Fortunately, this decision takes religion seriously, neither equating it with science nor limiting it solely to the dominant Christian model.

The case arose in the mid-1970s when five New Jersey public high schools decided to offer an elective course called the Science of Creative Intelligence—Transcendental Meditation.[77] The course used a textbook developed by the Maharishi Mahesh Yogi. The key to the course was teaching students to engage in transcendental meditation in order to "perceive the full potential of their lives."[78] In order to meditate in the proper fashion, each student attended a ceremony called a "puja," to which he or she was required to bring some fruit, flowers, and a white handkerchief.[79] At the puja, the student received a personal mantra, a sound aid used while meditating.[80]

Proponents of this program argued that it was a secular method for improving the well-being of students. They said that no religious element is present, any more than it is in a physical education class that improves a student's bodily health.[81] The federal courts found, however, that this transcendental meditation program was a religious activity and that it therefore could not be offered in the public schools.[82] Judge Arlin Adams wrote a lengthy concurring opinion that canvassed the precedents and relevant literature and then set forth the factors that should be considered in deciding whether an activity was religious.[83] Adams agreed that the New Jersey program was religious, but more important, his approach has been widely cited by other federal and state courts.[84] Whether the United States Supreme Court would follow Adams's analysis is unclear, but it seems quite likely that they would at least consider it if they ever had to define religion under the First Amendment.

Adams identified three factors that he considered relevant in deciding whether an activity or belief system was religious. First, he said that religious ideas address "fundamental" or "ultimate" questions. They concern "the meaning of life and death, man's role in the Universe, the proper moral code of right and wrong."[85]

The second factor is comprehensiveness. Adams argued, "A religion is not generally confined to one question or one moral teaching; it has a broader scope. It lays claim to an ultimate and comprehensive 'truth.'"[86] Thus, he easily disposed of the idea that a scientific idea is a religion, noting that "the so-called 'Big Bang' theory, an astronomical interpretation of the creation of the universe, may be said to answer an 'ultimate' question, but it is not, by itself, a 'religious' idea."[87]

Finally, Adams said the courts should consider whether the belief system in question includes any formal, external signs that might be analogized to traditional religions.[88] Although outward signs are not required for religious faith, they can be important evidence of whether religion is present. Adams identified "formal services, ceremonial functions, the existence of clergy, structure and organization, efforts at propagation, observation of holidays," and the like as relevant here.[89] Throughout his enterprise, Adams was determined to show that "[n]ew and different [faiths] are entitled to the same sort of treatment as the traditional forms."[90]

Applying these tests to transcendental meditation, Adams noted that the textbook saw its approach as "at the basis of all growth and progress . . . the basis of everything."[91] It thus treated ultimate concerns, and although not as comprehensive as some faiths, it did present what it regarded as "*the* way . . . to full self realization and oneness with the underlying reality of the universe."[92] Finally, the puja ceremony was similar to traditional religious rites.[93] Thus, for all of these reasons, even though transcendental meditation was not a theistic religion, it was a religion for purposes of the Constitution.

ACCOMMODATION IN PRACTICE

A sensitivity to the importance of religion has guided the judiciary's emphasis on the accommodation of faith. As Judge Adams wrote, "The First Amendment demonstrates a specific solicitude for religion because religious ideas are in many ways more important than other ideas."[94] Non-establishment and free exercise protect religion from government interference, while allowing it to flourish in the private sphere.

As we have seen in the case of a religious group being allowed to use a controlled substance in its rituals, the Supreme Court gives legislatures considerable leeway in deciding whether to accommodate religious practices that otherwise would violate the law. The origins and current implementation of this idea give a clear picture of the real state of religious freedom in the United States today. This is not a country where the most important religious question is whether Frosty the Snowman has to guard a Christmas display. Those cases are costly diversions. Real religious freedom turns on far more fundamental questions.

The first major case in which the Supreme Court allowed a legislative accommodation against the claim that it established religion set the stage for the modern approach. The issue arose years ago in the important setting of employment law.[95] Title VII of the Civil Rights Act of 1964 prohibits discrimination in employment on the basis of religion.[96] If a department store or accounting firm is advertising for employees, the company cannot say, "No Jews need apply." In its original form, this statute had an understandable exemption for religious employers hiring people to perform religious activities. So a Methodist church seeking a new minister could say, "No Jews need apply."[97]

In 1972, Title VII was amended to apply this exemption to all activities of religious organizations.[98] Senator Sam Ervin, who sponsored the amendment, said it was designed to "take the political hands of Caesar off of the institutions of God, where they have no place to be."[99] Under this amendment, a gift shop in a church could hire only church members if it so desired. But was the amendment constitutional, or did it go too far in allowing discrimination in hiring on the basis of religion?

The Supreme Court case arose when a nonprofit gymnasium run by the Church of Jesus Christ of Latter-Day Saints, sometimes called the LDS or Mormon Church, discharged a building engineer because he did not qualify for a temple recommend, that is, a certificate that he is a member of the Church eligible to attend its temples.[100] The Church believed it could not fulfill its religious mission if it could not control who worked in its facilities. The engineer brought suit, claiming that Title VII's allowing a church, but not a secular employer, to discriminate in hiring was an unconstitutional establishment of religion.[101]

In 1987, every member of the Supreme Court rejected the engineer's challenge. They upheld Congress's accommodation of religious employers who felt the need to hire people who shared the same religious beliefs. Congress was not required to make this accommodation, but they were free to do so. In his opinion for the Court, Justice Byron White said that the legislature is free "to alleviate significant governmental interference with the ability of religious organizations to define and carry out their religious missions. . . . Where, as here, government acts with the proper purpose of lifting a regulation that burdens the exercise of religion, we see no reason to require that the exemption comes packaged with benefits to secular entities."[102]

In recent years, the Court has followed this lead, allowing the legislatures room to maneuver in deciding whether to accommodate religious exercise. Legislatures are still bound at the extremes: they cannot single out religion for punishment, nor can they impose religious beliefs on the unwilling. But between the extremes, they can attempt to navigate safe passage between non-establishment and free exercise principles.

Two recent cases show the Court's willingness to support the legislature in both directions. In the first, the legislature made a choice that displeased some religious leaders; in the second, the choice angered some secular authorities. In both cases, the Court upheld efforts to preserve the distinctive American balance between free exercise and non-establishment.

The case that angered some supporters of religion concerned the Promise Scholarship Program created by the State of Washington.[103] Under this program, academically gifted students could receive about fifteen hundred dollars per year from the state to defray the costs of college. A Promise Scholarship winner had to attend college in Washington. The money could be used for any accredited school, including private religious schools, but it was not available if the student planned to study devotional theology.[104] Joshua Davey, who qualified for a Promise Scholarship, chose to attend Northwest College, a private, Christian school, in order to receive the training necessary to become a church pastor. When he learned that he could not use the money because of his course of study, he sued, claiming a violation of his free exercise and other rights.[105]

In the United States Supreme Court in 2004, Chief Justice Rehnquist wrote the opinion for seven justices rejecting Joshua's claim.[106] Rehnquist noted that, because the Court had upheld voucher programs, Washington could have allowed scholarship recipients to use their money for any course of study at all. In such a case, Joshua's choice to study for the ministry would be his choice, not that of the state.[107] But although Washington could have allowed Joshua to apply his money to his pastoral training without violating the Establishment Clause, it was not required to do so. This was state money, after all. No one was preventing Joshua from studying anything he liked. The State of Washington, like many others, has long been troubled by using taxpayer money to fund the clergy, directly or indirectly.[108] Free exercise does not mandate that Washington affirmatively spend money in the manner Joshua sought.

One year later, legislative discretion was exercised in the opposite direction, and once again it was upheld. A federal statute mandated that state prison officials allow inmates to exercise their religions unless a compelling interest, such as maintaining order in the prisons, made such exercise unacceptable.[109] The State of Ohio argued that this was a special favor for religion that violated the Establishment Clause. After all, the State argued, most inmate activities, including nonreligious political gatherings, can be regulated by the warden in any way that is reasonable—no one says that the warden's regulations typically have to serve a compelling interest.[110]

The Supreme Court agreed that the federal statute gave special deference to the religious practices of inmates, but it held, in a unanimous 2005 opinion written by Justice Ginsburg, that this did not violate the Establishment Clause. Congress was accommodating the free exercise of inmates by using the compelling state interest test, just as Congress had done in other areas involving religion.[111] Congress was not required to give inmate religious exercise this special freedom, but it was free to do so. This statute was not passed by accident—many in Congress believe that religion in prison is one of the best ways to avoid recidivism.

These cases reflect a common theme. There is, as the Court put it, "room for play in the joints" between the Free Exercise and Establishment Clauses.[112] If the legislature does not stray too far in either direction, it is carrying out the vital role of preserving America's unique approach to the relationship between church and state.

KEEPING THE COURTS OUT OF
INTERNAL CHURCH DISPUTES

The final piece in the relationship between the government and religion is the set of legal doctrines designed to keep the courts away from resolving internal church disputes. Every court in the United States today agrees that judges should not try to figure out the merits of religious matters that divide parishioners. Remarkably enough, often churches themselves continue to press these matters in court. Once again, there are religious leaders who do not realize the high cost of forcing their faith into the judicial arena. Our current legal doctrines designed to keep courts away from theology seem obvious and uncontroversial. But here as elsewhere the approach taken in the United States represents a distinctive point of view that has greatly strengthened the role of religion in America.

If American courts had followed the British common law, the situation would be very different. In an 1817 British decision involving charitable trusts, Lord Eldon held that assets held in trust for a church had to be used to support the church doctrines in place at the time the contributions were made.[113] And who would decide what those doctrines were? Lord Eldon found that this was his job, because it is "the duty of the Court in such cases to inquire and decide for itself . . . what is the true standard of faith in the church organization, and which of the contending parties before the Court holds to this standard."[114]

Perhaps in an England where the judges and the parties were all members of the Church of England, and the judges could be relied on to know church doctrine, this approach makes some sense. But in the United States, where religious diversity, even within the Christian faith, is the norm, and where judges are hardly experts on religion, Lord Eldon's approach makes no sense at all. The United States Supreme Court has rejected Lord Eldon's rule and instead taken the view that the Court should defer to appropriate church authorities on matters of religious doctrine.

The current approach of the Supreme Court was set forth in the 1979 decision in *Jones v. Wolf,* which grew out of a property dispute within the Presbyterian Church in Macon, Georgia.[115] The general framework set forth in the *Jones* case remains in place today. The problem in Georgia grew out of a split in the Presbyterian Church. In the 1970s, a group called the Presbyterian Church in America split off from the mainstream Presbyterian Church. The new group believed that the mainstream church had become too liberal by ordaining women and by failing to adhere to the inerrancy of scripture.[116] The Vineville Presbyterian Church in Macon had been organized in 1904. In 1973, a majority of its members, including the pastor, decided to separate from the mainstream church and join the more conservative Presbyterian Church in America. A dispute arose as to who owned the church property, the mainstream group or the more conservative local Vineville group.[117]

In approaching problems of this type, courts begin by looking at the structure of the religious group in question. Some groups, such as the Baptists, have a congregational structure.[118] Each local congregation is self-governing. Larger Baptist conferences may help promote shared goals, but they do not control the local groups. With religions of that type, the courts attempt to work out property disputes and the like by treating the church like any voluntary association and thus looking to its charters, deeds, and so on. The goal is to apply neutral legal principles without taking sides in any doctrinal split. Other religious groups are hierarchical in structure. In this arrangement final decisions are made by a centralized body or individual who heads the whole church. The Catholic Church, for example, is hierarchical, with ultimate power residing in Rome. Of course, a hierarchical church might choose to delegate decisions in certain areas to regional or local bodies.

The Presbyterian Church is hierarchical, and the leadership of the central, mainstream authority claimed that it therefore owned the property in dispute in Macon, Georgia.[119] But the local, breakaway group said that Presbyterian practice did not work that way—even though the Presbyterian Church is generally hierarchical, the deed to the church property in Georgia and relevant church documents revealed that the local membership owned the disputed property.[120] The Georgia courts examined the deed and the church documents and, applying neutral principles of law, concluded that the local breakaway church owned the property.[121] The United States Supreme Court affirmed this decision.

The Supreme Court reasoned that state courts had a choice in cases like this. They could simply defer to the hierarchy of the mainstream church, or they could, as the Georgia court had done, apply neutral principles of law to deeds and the like and rule accordingly.[122] In neither case was the court to intrude into matters of church doctrine. In other words, no court was to decide who was correct as a matter of church law on the question of the ordination of women.[123] The Supreme Court majority's willingness to accept the neutral principles approach in the case of a hierarchical church drew a dissent from four justices. The dissenters would have always deferred to the top figures in a hierarchical church.[124]

But the Supreme Court majority emphasized that a church could deal with this problem in advance by its drafting of relevant church documents and deeds.[125] In the case of the Macon church, those instruments vested authority in the local group. If that is not the real policy of the main body of the Presbyterian Church, the church should clarify its policy. Justice Blackmun's opinion for the majority of the Supreme Court emphasized in several places that proper drafting will clarify matters and keep the courts out. He wrote that through such drafting "religious societies can specify what is to happen to church property in the event of a particular contingency or what religious body will determine the ownership in the event of a schism or doctrinal controversy."[126]

In theory, every religious group in America has the ability to restrict the role of secular courts, a goal strongly endorsed by the courts themselves. Ordinary contracts and deeds can make clear who within the church gets what when property disputes arise. Yet every year a remarkable number of cases arise in hierarchical churches over matters such as who owns the building when the central authority closes a local church or when a local group breaks away because of a doctrinal dispute.[127] Sometimes the documents are vague, and sometimes, even when the underlying documents are quite clear, one group or another is eager to go to court in order to work out a church problem in the public arena. Most amazing of all are those cases where a church cannot resolve a leadership question internally so plays out a theological dispute in the courts and the newspapers. It is bad enough to have to litigate over who owns a building. It is really unsettling to turn to secular courts to decide who leads your church.

Yet these cases continue to arise. A remarkable example concerned the question of who should be the rector of the Episcopal parish in Accokeek, Maryland.[128] In 2000, a local church, the Vestry of St. John's in Accokeek, selected Father Samuel L. Edwards to be its rector. But the bishop of the Episcopal Diocese of Washington, Jane Holmes Dixon, declined to allow Father Edwards to assume this position.[129] Edwards nonetheless began to serve as rector, and when Bishop Dixon visited the parish to officiate in his place, the local members and Father Edwards refused to permit her to enter the church.[130]

Bishop Dixon filed suit in federal court and eventually won a judgment preventing Father Edwards from serving as rector. The trial and appellate courts reasoned that the Episcopal Church was hierarchical and that church law made clear that the bishop of the diocese had the power to approve or disapprove a vestry's choice for rector.[131] The underlying dispute, which the courts avoided, was a nasty one. Father Edwards was an opponent of changes in the Episcopal Church, having said, for example, that "the machinery of the Church is hell-bound" and that he could not guarantee he could obey the instruction of a female bishop.[132]

Nonetheless, it is surprising and more than a little troubling that, according to the appellate court's opinion, when Bishop Dixon was denied the ability to preside at a service at the Vestry of St. John's, she "promptly filed this civil action."[133] Indeed, it appears that both sides in this dispute were more interested in the glare of publicity than in attempting to resolve the matter internally. It is hard to see how that serves the interest of anyone in the Episcopal Church. The secular courts are neither ready, willing, nor able to work out religious doctrine, and it is a discouraging development when church members look to those courts when problems arise.

HEAD SCARVES IN AMERICAN SCHOOLS

When we step back and look at the legal relationship between church and state in America as a whole, we see a framework that is conducive to the flourishing of religion. The system, if allowed to work, nurtures real faith. Despite the disagreements that often seize the headlines, there are vital areas of shared purpose. When we look now at students wearing religious garb in American public schools, the picture of religious freedom in America comes into focus. It is not a story of any one legal doctrine or political point of view. Liberals and conservatives alike disagree with the French decision to forbid their students from wearing religious apparel.[134] And neither liberals nor conservatives lobby for the Iranian rule that every student be required to wear the trappings of faith.

Throughout America today, students often wear visible symbols of their faith when they go to public school. They may believe their religion requires them to do so, or they may simply do it as a matter of personal preference. But in most cases, there is simply no problem. A student may wear a cross, or a Star of David, or a head scarf, and classes go on as usual. But this is a large country with thousands of school districts, each with its own policies and concerns, and at times a controversy concerning religious apparel arises. In the bulk of these cases, the student wins the right to continue his or her religious expression. It is, after all, the private expression of the student that is involved, not the words of the government, and students do not surrender all of their rights at the schoolhouse door.

In 2004, the same year the French were banning head scarves in public schools, the Muskogee, Oklahoma, School District agreed to allow an eleven-year-old Muslim student, Nashala Hearn, to wear a head scarf to class. The case had attracted national attention because Muskogee had initially suspended Nashala for wearing the scarf.[135] Muskogee has a "no head covering" dress code designed to curb gang activity.[136] At first, the school district declined to make an exception for Nashala, even though she clearly was not promoting gang colors.[137] As the Supreme Court noted in the *hoasca* case, bureaucrats are instinctively drawn to the "if I make an exception for you, I'll have to make one for everybody" line of argument.

However, our law and our values do make an exception for the free exercise of religion. The reaction to the Muskogee decision was dramatic. Not only did civil liberties and religious freedom groups line up behind the student and bring a lawsuit on her behalf but the United States Justice Department agreed that her rights had been violated.[138] Oklahoma has a religious freedom act that makes the state grant religious exemptions unless there is a compelling reason not to.[139] In the end, Muskogee saw the handwriting on the wall and settled the lawsuit, agreeing not only to allow Nashala Hearn to wear her head scarf but to change its policies to generally permit school attire that is worn for religious reasons.[140]

This sort of conflict had arisen before in the context of other religious practices. In 1997, David Chalifoux and Jerry Robinson, students at New Caney High School, a public school in Texas, began wearing white plastic rosaries, a string of beads with a crucifix attached to the center, on the outside of their shirts in order to communicate their Catholic faith to others.[141] The school told them they had to wear the rosaries inside their shirts, since the beads were considered "gang-related apparel."[142] When the dispute went to court, the students won the right to wear their Christian symbols on the outside of their shirts. The judge threw the book at the school district, not only citing the students' free speech rights and free exercise rights but stressing that there was no evidence these students had gang connections and criticizing the "gang-related apparel" rule as overly broad.[143]

Now these cases may seem like relatively easy examples of overly zealous school officials misapplying rules aimed at gangs. But even in closer cases, the religious freedom of students has won out.

In the Sikh religion, which arose in India, it is an article of faith that baptized members wear a kirpan—a small ceremonial knife. In 1994, the Livingstone School District in northern California sought to ban Sikh students from wearing the kirpan on safety grounds.[144] Obviously, public schools can ban weapons. But the kirpan need not pose a threat, and indeed, the school district had not shown that kirpans had been involved in any violence.

After a lawsuit began, a settlement was reached in which Sikh students could continue to wear the kirpan. Under the agreement, the kirpan blade was to be dulled, no longer than 2.5 inches, sewn into a sheath, and further secured in a cloth pouch that the Sikh community designed to accommodate the school's concerns over safety.[145] In 2005, a similar agreement allowed Amandeep Singh, a Sikh ninth-grader, to wear a kirpan to Woodlands High School in Hartsdale, New York.[146]

When litigation arises about public displays of quasi-religious symbols on town squares every December, you can count on the American Civil Liberties Union to oppose the displays, and the Becket Fund for Religious Liberty to be on the other side, supporting the town government. It is worth noting that when meaningful religious expression by young people is at stake, as in these kirpan cases, the American Civil Liberties Union and the Becket Fund for Religious Liberty are on the same side—the side of the students and religious liberty.[147] Meaningful religious freedom in America is a widely and deeply held value.

THE PERILS OF FORCING GOVERNMENT
AND RELIGION INTO THE SAME BED

Imagine if you walked into church one Sunday and saw a brand-new plaque on the wall that read:

To all free men of our kingdom, we have granted for us and our heirs for ever, all the liberties written out below, to have and to keep for them and their heirs, of us and our heirs:

For so long as a guardian has guardianship of such land, he shall maintain the houses, parks, fish preserves, ponds, mills, and everything else pertaining to it, for the revenues of the land itself.

At her husband's death, a widow may have her marriage portion and inheritance at once and without trouble. She shall pay nothing for her dower, marriage portion, or any inheritance that she and her husband held jointly on the day of his death.

If anyone who has borrowed a sum of money from Jews dies before the debt has been repaid, his heir shall pay no interest on the debt for so long as he remains under age.

For a trivial offence, a free man shall be fined only in proportion to the degree of his offence, and for a serious offence correspondingly, but not so heavily as to deprive him of his livelihood.

No free man shall be seized or imprisoned, or stripped of his rights or possessions, or outlawed or exiled, or deprived of his standing in any other way, nor will we proceed with force against him, or send others to do so, except by the lawful judgment of his equals or by the law of the land.

To no one will we sell, or no one deny or delay right or justice.

All evil customs relating to forests and warrens, foresters, warreners, sheriffs and their servants, or riverbanks and their wardens, are at once to be investigated in every county by twelve sworn knights of the county, and within forty days of their enquiry the evil customs are to be abolished completely and irrevocably.

No one shall be arrested or imprisoned on the appeal of a woman for the death of any person except her husband.

After reading this plaque on your church wall, you might well inquire as to what it is and why it is there. Imagine that you learn that leaders of your town government posted it. They were very proud of the philosophy of government they followed and wanted you to acknowledge its role in the society in which you live. They sought to post a fundamental document that served as an early basis for their philosophy, so they chose the Magna Carta, which was issued in AD 1215.[148]

Would reading this plaque on your church wall cause you to think more highly of the secular government? Or would you resent the intrusion into your place of worship? Does the plaque convey the central features of American law? Or does it read as though the people posting it did not really pay attention to what it said?

I can imagine that if the leaders of a town government were to debate whether to post the Magna Carta in a local church, some of them would argue that this was a really bad idea. They would be right. The Magna Carta was written in Latin, and the translation above is necessarily imprecise. The complete Magna Carta is too long to put on a plaque, so the version above is edited. Moreover, the Magna Carta was reissued several times in different forms, and it contained many provisions, such as those relating to Jews and women, that do not reflect the views of the American government today.[149]

All of this could be said about the Ten Commandments plaques that some would put in government buildings today. What is posted is a translation (is it "thou shalt not kill" or "thou shalt not murder"?), it is edited (much about the Sabbath is generally left out), you are choosing one version of the two that appear in the Bible (contrast the Exodus and Deuteronomy versions), and it contains language that many religious people do not regard as binding today ("the iniquity of the fathers" is visited on the children for three and four generations).

It is true that the Magna Carta did represent an extraordinarily important early effort to limit the king of England and that it is an ancestor of many rights we hold dear.[150] But it is impossible to capture all of that on a plaque. The town government would be better served by teaching about American law thoroughly and substantively in appropriate settings. Public schools might be a good place to start.

The Ten Commandments is a remarkably influential early code of Jewish law and is an ancestor of much later thinking in Jewish, Christian, and other traditions. However, you cannot understand it by reading a plaque in a public building. It should be studied thoroughly and substantively in appropriate settings. Churches and synagogues might be a good place to start.

The important question is not the legality of posting these plaques. The important question is whether it is wise to do so, and the answer is no. The problem is not simply the dangers inherent in reducing a serious document to a symbol so edited, translated, and ripped out of context as to be meaningless. The problem is also that the intrusion of this symbol into another domain represents a power play, not an effort at teaching or understanding. And power plays often boomerang in the long run.

Suppose your child attends a Sunday School class where he or she reads a passage in the Book of Matthew in which Jesus teaches that one of the most important commandments is "Love thy neighbor as thyself." The teacher then interrupts the class to read a disclaimer insisted on by the town government: "This passage presents a controversial theory. The Book of Matthew cannot explain scientific proof that love is governed by the presence of the hormones oxytocin and vasopressin. The state of being in love is similar to cocaine addiction." Perhaps the town government believed that children in church schools were being misled about the importance of science, and they wanted to remedy the situation. Have they come up with a good plan? Will respect for science soar whenever this disclaimer is read?

Of course, perhaps the town government is simply engaged in a power play. You think religion is important, but the government thinks science is more important and is going to cram that idea down your throat. In the long run, this is a misguided strategy. This imaginary disclaimer suffers from all of the defects of the very real intelligent design disclaimer that some have tried to force into public school science classes. Intelligent design misrepresents God as a second-rate engineer, leaving out matters of morality and faith. A bald statement of "scientific proof" that certain hormones govern love misrepresents science as a set of conclusions, leaving out the central process of carefully formulating and testing a limited hypothesis.[151]

My examples of forcing the Magna Carta and scientific definitions of love into church are hypothetical. In reality, secular leaders realize that this approach is not only illegal and unworkable but unwise. It would be a confession of weakness that they could not make their case in their own forum and would likely lead to a loss of support for their goals. But forcing the Ten Commandments and religious disclaimers about evolution into the public square is not hypothetical. Regrettably, some religious leaders do not realize that this approach is a confession of weakness that they cannot make their case in church and at home, and it is likely to lead in the long run to a loss of support for their goals.

There is a very old idea here that we need to remember from time to time. When church and state get into bed together, it is bad news for both of them. In discussing the separate roles of church and state, many are drawn to the metaphor of a wall between them. This image is obviously imperfect. Government leaders are allowed to discuss their faith. Clergy are not forbidden to praise their country. And in the American legal system, as we have seen, the law is allowed to accommodate the free exercise of religion under appropriate circumstances. But even if we look at the much-belabored "wall," we find a more subtle idea than is sometimes supposed. Thomas Jefferson, who wrote in 1802 that the First Amendment created "a wall of separation between church and State,"[152] had a sharp concern that established religion would stifle free inquiry. As he wrote some years before his "wall" reference:

Galileo was sent to the Inquisition for affirming that the earth was a sphere; the government had declared it to be as flat as a trencher, and Galileo was obliged to abjure his error. This error, however, at length prevailed, [and] the earth became a globe. . . . [T]he Newtonian principle of gravitation is now more firmly established, on the basis of reason, than it would be were the government to step in, and to make it an article of necessary faith.[153]

On the other hand, Roger Williams used the wall metaphor a century and a half before Jefferson to demonstrate the opposite danger: religion is imperiled when it falls into the clutches of the state. Williams was a devout Christian who fled the Puritan authorities in charge of the seventeenth-century Massachusetts Bay Colony after they charged him with heresy. He then founded the colony of Rhode Island, which had no established church and recognized religious freedom. Williams wrote: "When they have opened a gap in the hedge or wall of separation between the garden of the church, and the wilderness of the world, God hath ever broken down the wall itself, removed the Candlestick, etc., and made his garden a wilderness, as at this day."[154]

So it was the garden of the church that was at risk when church and state were not separated. The destruction of that garden is depicted quite dramatically in this passage. When Williams said that "the Candlestick" is removed from the church, he had a very specific image in mind. The King James translation of the Book of Exodus translates *menorah*—the original seven-branched candelabrum God ordered the Jews in the desert to make from gold—as "candlestick." Williams was evoking the image of the destruction of the Temple with the pagan Roman soldiers carrying off the menorah.[155] As we have seen, that image has been obliterated for many today by the far less important Chanukah menorah, but it was quite vivid in the seventeenth century to Roger Williams. We would be wise to learn from both Thomas Jefferson and Roger Williams. Forcing religion into the public square will result in Pyrrhic victories at best.

The unique American blend of free exercise and non-establishment— our insistence on avoiding both intolerant secularism and suffocating theocracy—should be a source of pride. We all learn in school that the settlers of this country came so that they could practice their religions freely. It is worth remembering that people are still coming to America for the same reason.

To this day, Christians from Asia, Jews from Russia, Muslims from India, and many others come to follow their faith in peace. They do not come here because Frosty the Snowman appears on a town square, standing guard next to a Christmas tree and a nine-branched Chanukah menorah. They come to practice meaningful religion in a free society.

CHAPTER 6

Conclusion

I REALIZE THAT RELIGION does not reside in a hermetically sealed compartment separate from the rest of American society. The workings of government inevitably bear on the lives of churches and churchgoers. The advances of modern science shape our perception of the world. And popular culture washes over everything, affecting public discourse and private morality alike. Even the Amish have to struggle to maintain a simple life, untouched by modern society. Most of us have no desire to separate ourselves as the Amish do. We want to participate in the secular world without losing our spiritual dimension.

But the powerful pressures of government, science, and culture make the lessons I am arguing for more, not less, vital. The symbols of religious faith will rapidly lose their importance, and their deeper teachings will lose their distinctive value, if religion fails to stand up for its vital role as a guardian of timeless faith and values.

It is a needless and costly surrender when the religious elements of Christmas and Chanukah are stripped away for the dubious honor of standing on government land. It is a ludicrous distortion when God is replaced by the second-rate engineer of "intelligent design" so that an unrecognizable version of religion can make its way into the hallowed halls of ninth-grade biology. And it is a complete victory for the worst elements of popular culture when people of faith reduce the Ten Commandments to the symbolic status of the Nike Swoosh and demand that Christmas become ever more closely tied to December shopping sprees.

What message does religion send when it pays this price to force itself into the public square? It is a message of insecurity and self-doubt. We have seen how costly and misguided it would be if government tried to force the posting of the Magna Carta in every church or if scientists insisted that teachings of Christian love be accompanied by disclaimers discussing the biochemical roots of emotions. But note that governments and scientists do not push for these policies. They have enough faith in what they stand for to make their case in their own arenas.

The bleached faith we see all around us is not the inevitable product of American law. It is the result of mistaken policy choices. True religious faith flourishes in America, fully protected by our Constitution and traditions. People of all faiths can worship, proselytize, and take political commitments shaped by their religious beliefs into public debate. They can educate their children in pervasively religious schools or in their own homes. They can display real religious symbols on their property.

It is not by chance that America has a far more religious population than the nations of Western Europe. Our commitments to free exercise, non-establishment, free speech, and due process provide the sort of protection for religion that is the envy of people around the world. But the future of religion in America is threatened when it surrenders to government, science, and popular culture by watering down its symbols and teachings. That surrender can be and should be resisted by people of faith throughout the United States.

Notes

CHAPTER 2

1. See, e.g., *Requiring the Display of the Ten Commandments in the Hall of the House of Representatives and the Chamber of the Senate*, 109 H. Con. Res. 11, 109th Cong. (2005); *A Bill to Defend the Ten Commandments*, H.R. 2045, 108th Cong. (2003); see also John Rivera, "Push for Posting 10 Commandments Gaining in States"; "Hang Ten" Campaign Seeks to Bypass Church-State Issue, *Baltimore Sun*, Feb. 14, 2000, 1A; Larry Copeland, "Morality Makes a Stand," *USA Today*, Mar. 30, 2000, A01; see generally, Tarik Abdel-Monem, Note, "Posting the Ten Commandments as a Historical Document in Public Schools," *Iowa Law Review* 87 (2002): 1023, 1043–46.

2. *McCreary County, Kentucky v. American Civil Liberties Union*, 125 S. Ct. 2722, 2731 (2005).

3. Ibid. at 2739.

4. Ibid. at 2731.

5. See, e.g., *Van Orden v. Perry*, 125 S. Ct. 2854 (2005); *McCreary*, 125 S. Ct. 2722 (2005); *Stone v. Graham*, 449 U.S. 39 (1980); *Books v. City of Elkhart*, 235 F.3d 292, 307 (7th Cir. 2000).

6. See, e.g., Robert Alter, *The Five Books of Moses: A Translation with Commentary*, XVI (2004) ("The King James Version [Has] a Shaky Sense of Hebrew"); James R. White, *The King James Only Controversy* (1995); D. A. Carson, *The King James Version Debate: A Plea for Realism* (1979).

7. On Catholic translations, see Michael W. McConnell, *Religion and the Constitution*, 357 (2d ed., 2006) (quoting Jeffries and Ryan); on Jewish translations, see Elliot N. Dorff, "Symposium on Cloning: Human Cloning: A Jewish Perspective," *Southern California Interdisciplinary Law Journal* 8 (1998): 117, 121 n. 2.

8. *The Ten Commandments*, app. (William P. Brown ed., 2004); Paul Finkelman, "The Ten Commandments on the Courthouse Lawn and Elsewhere," *Fordham Law Review* 73 (2005): 1477, 1485–88.

9. Brown, *Ten Commandments*, app.

10. A. Powell Davies, *The Ten Commandments*, 69–70 (1956).

11. Ibid., 26.

12. See also Exodus 25:1–40 (King James).

13. See generally, Brown, *Ten Commandments*, 2 n. 2; George R. Berry, "The Ritual Decalogue," *Journal of Biblical Literature* 44 (1925): 39.

14. Deuteronomy 5:6–21 (King James).

15. John C. Holbert, *The Ten Commandments*, 49–59 (2002).

16. See generally, J. J. Stamm and M. E. Andrew, *The Ten Commandments in Recent Research*, 13 (M. E. Andrew trans., 1967) (orig. pub. 1962); Anthony Phillips, *Ancient Israel's Criminal Law: A New Approach to the Decalogue*, 14–36 (1970).

17. See, e.g., Richard E. Friedman, *The Bible with Sources Revealed* (2003).

18. *The Commandments: Sefer Ha-Mitzvoth of Maimonides*, 1:viii (Rabbi Dr. Charles B. Chavel ed., 1984) (orig. pub. 1967).

19. Ibid.

20. *Babylonian Talmud, Tractate Sanhedrin*, 86A (Jacob Neusner trans., 1984); Phillips, *Ancient Israel's Criminal Law*, 130–32.

21. Joseph Telushkin, *Jewish Literacy*, 509–10 (2001 reissue).

22. *Tractate Sanhedrin*, 56B.

23. Reginald Fuller, "The Decalogue in the New Testament," in *Ten Commandments* (Brown ed.), 33.

24. *New Catholic Encyclopedia*, 2d ed. (2003), s.v. "Images, Veneration of."

25. *Quaring v. Peterson*, 728 F.2d 1121 (8th Cir. 1984); affirmed by an equally divided court, 472 U.S. 478 (1985).

26. David C. Steinmetz, "The Reformation and the Ten Commandments," *Interpretation* 43 (1989): 256, 257; Holbert, *Ten Commandments*, 25.

27. *West Virginia State Board of Education v. Barnette*, 319 U.S. 624 (1943); see generally, David R. Manwaring, *Render unto Caesar: The Flag-Salute Controversy*, 30–34 (1962).

28. Bob DeWaay, "Generational Curses," http://www.inplainsite.org/html/generational_curses.html (last visited Nov. 10, 2006) (analyzing books such as Derek Prince, *Blessing or Curse: You Can Choose* [1990], which cite this biblical language to show that Christians are subjected to "generational curses that have detrimental effects on their lives," although authors such as Prince believe such curses can be alleviated).

29. Ibid. (citing Old and New Testament sources to show that this biblical language does "not support the idea that Christians are cursed because of the sins of their parents, grandparents, and great-grandparents").

30. Isaac Klein, *A Guide to Jewish Religious Practice*, 78 (1979).

31. Norman Wirzba, "Time Out: A Sabbath Sensibility," *Christian Century*, July 12, 2005, 24; Barbara Brown Taylor, "Sabbath Resistance," *Christian Century*, May 31, 2005, 122.

32. *Seventh-Day Adventists Answer Questions on Doctrine*, 129–32 (George R. Knight ed., ann. ed., 2003).

33. See generally, David B. Kopel, "The Torah and Self-Defense," *Pennsylvania State Law Review* 109 (2004): 17, 37–38.

34. See generally, Stamm and Andrew, *Ten Commandments*, 98.

35. See generally, Holbert, *Ten Commandments*, 75–85.

36. *McCreary*, 125 S. Ct. 2722, 2730 (2005).

37. *Van Orden*, 125 S. Ct. 2854, 2891 (Appendix to Opinion of Stevens, J.).

38. Ibid.; *McCreary*, 125 S. Ct. at 2730.

39. *Stone*, 449 U.S. 39 (1980). The account in this and the following paragraphs is drawn from the Court's opinion in *Stone*.

40. Ibid. at 39 n. 1.

41. Ibid. at 40.

42. *Stone v. Graham*, 599 S.W.2d 157, 160 (Sup. Ct. of Kentucky) (Lukowsky, J., for reversal).

43. Ibid.

44. Ibid. at 161.

45. Ibid. at 158 (Clayton, J.).

46. *Stone*, 449 U.S. 39 (1980).

47. Ibid. at 40.

48. See *Harris v. McRae*, 448 U.S. 297, 319 (1980).

49. See generally, Antonin Scalia, *A Matter of Interpretation* (1997).

50. *Stone*, 449 U.S. 39, 41–42 (1980).

51. Ibid. at 39.

52. Ibid. at 42.

53. Ibid.

54. Ibid. at 45 n. 2 (Rehnquist, J., dissenting).

55. Ibid. at 45–46.

56. Cynthia V. Ward, "Coercion and Choice under the Establishment Clause," *University of California, Davis Law Review* 39 (2006): 1621.

57. *Van Orden*, 125 S. Ct. 2854 (2005). The description in the following paragraphs is taken from the Court's opinion.

58. Ibid. at 2877 (Stevens, J., dissenting).

59. Ibid. at 2858.

60. Ibid. at 2873–74 (Stevens, J., dissenting).

61. *McCreary*, 125 S. Ct. 2722 (2005). The description in the following paragraphs is taken from the Court's opinion.

62. Ibid. at 2729.

63. Ibid. at 2731.

64. Ibid. at 2730.

65. Ibid. at 2730–31.

66. In fact, Stephen Prothero reports that "[i]n 2005, an enterprising journalist called up the ten cosponsors of an Alabama bill that sought to protect public displays of the Ten Commandments. Just one of those cosponsors could name all ten." Stephen Prothero, *Religious Literacy: What Every American Needs to Know—and Doesn't*, 30–31 (2007). Prothero finds a widespread lack of knowledge about religion and proposes various remedies, including individual study, classes in churches, synagogues, and the like; increased educational efforts in the media; and public school classes that study the Bible "academically." Ibid., 16, 17, 129. These proposals envision religious studies that are a far cry from the diluted and distorted image of religion that emerges when faith is pushed into the public square.

67. See, e.g., *American Civil Liberties Union of Ohio Foundation, Inc. v. Board of Com'rs of Lucas County, Ohio*, 444 F. Supp.2d 805 (N.D. Ohio 2006); *Twombly v. City of Fargo*, No. A3-02-137, 2005 WL 2401569 (D.N.D. 2005); *Card v. City of Everett*, No. C03-2385L, 2005 WL 2219382 (W.D. Wash. 2005); *Chambers v. City of Frederick*, 373 F. Supp.2d 567 (D. Md. 2005).

68. *McCreary*, 125 S. Ct. at 2727; *Van Orden*, 125 S. Ct. at 2873, 2891, 2892 (O'Connor, Souter, Stevens, J., dissenting).

69. *McCreary*, 125 S. Ct. at 2741; *Van Orden*, 125 S. Ct. at 2894 (Souter, J., dissenting).

70. *McCreary*, 125 S. Ct. at 2746 (O'Connor, J., concurring) (quoting *Wallace v. Jaffree*, 472 U.S. 38, 69 [1985]) (O'Connor, J., concurring in judgment).

71. *County of Allegheny v. American Civil Liberties Union*, 492 U.S. 573, 630, 635–36 (1989).

72. Ibid. at 635–36.

73. *McCreary*, 125 S. Ct. 2722 (2005); *Van Orden*, 125 S. Ct. 2854.

74. *McCreary*, 125 S. Ct. at 2759–61 (Scalia, J., dissenting); *Van Orden*, 125 S. Ct. at 2864.

75. *Van Orden*, 125 S. Ct. at 2861; *McCreary*, 125 S. Ct. at 2750 (Scalia, J., dissenting).

76. *Van Orden*, 125 S. Ct. at 2862.

77. Ibid. at 2863.

78. Ibid. at 2864 (Scalia, J., concurring).

79. *McCreary*, 125 S. Ct. at 2755 (Scalia, J., dissenting).

80. Richard W. Garnett, "Religion, Division, and the First Amendment," *Georgetown Law Journal* 94 (2006): 1667, 1701; Stephen E. Gottlieb, "Three Justices in Search of a Character: The Moral Agendas of Justices O'Connor, Scalia and Kennedy," *Rutgers Law Review* 49 (1996): 219.

81. *Allegheny*, 492 U.S. 573, 664 (1989) (Kennedy, J., concurring and dissenting in part).

82. *Allegheny*, 492 U.S. at 661.

83. *Van Orden*, 125 S. Ct. at 2871 (Breyer, J., concurring).

84. Ibid. at 2869.

85. Ibid. at 2870.

86. Ibid. at 2871.

87. Ibid. Erwin Chemerinsky, a scholar who represented Thomas Van Orden in the Texas case, criticizes Justice Breyer's conclusion that the Texas display did not endorse religion in "Symposium: Why Justice Breyer Was Wrong in *Van Orden v. Perry*," *William & Mary Bill of Rights Journal* 14 (2005): 1. As part of his larger critique of Supreme Court religion clause jurisprudence, Frank Ravitch also finds fault with Breyer's reasoning in *Masters of Illusion: The Supreme Court and the Religion Clauses*, 131–32 (2007).

88. See, e.g., *McCreary*, 125 S. Ct. at 2755 (Scalia, J., dissenting).

89. E.g., "Brief for the American Jewish Congress, on Behalf of Itself, the American Jewish Committee, Americans for Religious Liberty, Jewish Council on Public Affairs, Union for Reform Judaism and the Central Conference of American Rabbis, as Amici Curiae Supporting Petitioner, Van Orden," 125 S. Ct. 2854 (2005) (No. 03-1500); "Brief of Baptist Joint Committee and the Interfaith Alliance Foundation as Amici Curiae in Support of Petitioner, Brief of Baptist Joint Committee and the Interfaith Alliance Foundation as Amici Curiae supporting Petitioner, Van Orden," 125 S. Ct. 2854 (No. 03-1500).

90. See, e.g., Andrew Oldenquist, "Ten Commandments Are Problematical If All Beliefs Are to Be Respected," *Columbus Dispatch*, Mar. 7, 2005, 9A.

91. "Briefing Book: News and Views from the Louisiana Capitol," New Orleans *Times-Picayune*, July 2, 2006, 6.

92. Manwaring, *Render unto Caesar*, 30–34. The account in this and following paragraphs is drawn from Manwaring's book, as well as the Court's decisions in *Minersville School Dist. v. Gobitis*, 310 U.S. 586 (1940) and *West Virginia State Board of Education v. Barnette*, 319 U.S. 624 (1943).

93. The history of the Pledge of Allegiance is discussed in Chapter 5 of this book.

94. *Gobitis*, 310 U.S. 586 (1940). The account in this and the following paragraph is drawn from the Court's decision in *Gobitis*.

95. Ibid. at 600.

96. Manwaring, *Render unto Caesar*, 187–95. The account in this and the following paragraph is drawn from the Manwaring book and from the Court's decision in *West Virginia State Board of Education v. Barnette*, 319 U.S. 624 (1943).

97. *Barnette*, 319 U.S. 624 (1943). The account in this and the following paragraph is drawn from the Court's opinion in *Barnette*.

98. Ibid. at 642.

99. Todd D. Rakoff, *A Time for Every Purpose: Law and the Balance of Life*, 36 (2002).

100. Ibid., 35.

101. 18 *Purdon's Pennsylvania Statutes Annotated* § 4699.4 (quoted in *Two Guys from Harrison-Allentown, Inc. v. McGinley*, 366 U.S. 582, 585 [1961]).

102. Rakoff, *A Time for Every Purpose*, 35.

103. *McGowan v. State of Md.*, 366 U.S. 420 (1961); *Two Guys From Harrison-Allentown*, 366 U.S. 582 (1961); *Braunfield v. Brown*, 366 U.S. 599 (1961); *Gallagher v. Crown Kosher Super Market*, 366 U.S. 617 (1961). This and the following paragraphs are drawn from these Supreme Court opinions.

104. Ibid. This account continues to be drawn from these four opinions.

105. *McGowan*, 366 U.S. at 446.

106. Ibid.

107. Ibid. at 452.

108. *Braunfield*, 366 U.S. at 606.

109. Ibid.

110. *McGowan*, 366 U.S. at 450.

111. Rakoff, *A Time for Every Purpose*, 48–49.

CHAPTER 3

1. See, e.g., Ernst Mayr, *One Long Argument*, 1 (1991).

2. *The Darwin Reader*, 70–113 (Mark Ridley ed., 1987).

3. Genesis 1:1–31 (King James).

4. See *McLean v. Ark. Bd. of Educ.*, 529 F. Supp. 1255, 1268 (E.D. Ark. 1982).

5. Joshua 10:12–13 (King James).

6. Gerald L. Schroeder, *Genesis and the Big Bang: The Discovery of Harmony between Modern Science and the Bible* (1990); Pope John Paul II, "Message to Pontifical Academy of Sciences," Oct. 22, 1996, reprinted in *Origins* 26 (Nov. 14, 1996): 349, http://www.cin.org/jp2evolu.html (last visited Aug. 7, 2006).

7. See, e.g., Francis S. Collins, *The Language of God: A Scientist Presents Evidence for Belief* (2006); Joan Roughgarden, *Evolution and Christian Faith: Reflections of an Evolutionary Biologist* (2006). Collins is a medical geneticist who headed the Human Genome Project; Roughgarden is a Stanford University biology professor.

8. See, e.g., Raymond A. Eve and Francis B. Harrold, *The Creationist Movement in Modern America*, 37–38 (1991).

9. *Scopes v. State*, 289 S.W. 363, 363 (Tenn. 1927).

10. *Daniel v. Waters*, 515 F.2d 485, 486 (6th Cir. 1975).

11. *Scopes*, 289 S.W. at 363.

12. Ibid. at 267.

13. Ibid.

14. *Epperson v. Arkansas*, 393 U.S. 97, 99 (1968).

15. Ibid.

16. Ibid. at 109.

17. Ibid. at 106.

18. Ibid. at 102.

19. *Daniel v. Waters*, 399 F. Supp. 510, 511–12 (Tenn. 1975).

20. *Daniel v. Waters*, 515 F.2d 485, 487 (6th Cir. 1975).

21. Ibid.

22. Ibid.

23. Ibid.

24. Ibid.

25. Ibid. at 489.

26. Ibid. at 491.

27. Phillip Freund, "The Golden Egg," in *Myths of Creation*, 55–59 (Peter Owen ed., 2003); Arlene Hirshfelder and Paulette Molin, *Encyclopedia of Native American Religions*, 59–61 (updated ed., 2000); David Adams Leeming and Margaret Adams Leeming, *Encyclopedia of Creation Myths* (1994).

28. I have previously discussed scientific creationism and related matters in Steven Goldberg, *Seduced by Science: How American Religion Has Lost Its Way*, 25–39 (1999).

29. John C. Whitcomb Jr. and Henry M. Morris, *The Genesis Flood* (1963) (orig. pub. 1961).

30. Ibid., 214–15.

31. Ibid., 329–30.

32. Ibid., 10, 81, 123, 353.

33. Steering Committee on Science and Creationism, National Academy of Sciences, *Science and Creationism: A View from the National Academy of Sciences* (1984).

34. Whitcomb and Morris, *The Genesis Flood*, xx–xxi.

35. Eve and Harrold, *Creationist Movement*, 50.

36. Dorothy Nelkin, *The Creation Controversy: Science or Scripture in the Schools*, 75 (1982).

37. *McLean v. Arkansas Bd. of Educ.*, 529 F. Supp. 1255, 1255 (E.D. Ark. 1982); *Arkansas Statutes Annotated* § 80-1663 (1981 Supp.) (repealed 1982).

38. *McLean*, 529 F. Supp., 1264.

39. Ibid. at 1256.

40. Ibid. at 1261.

41. Ibid. at 1266.

42. Ibid. at 1269.

43. *Edwards v. Aguillard*, 482 U.S. 578, 580 (1987).

44. Ibid.

45. Ibid. at 588.

46. Ibid. at 590.

47. Ibid. at 593.

48. Ibid.

49. Ibid. at 594.

50. *Kitzmiller v. Dover Area Sch. Dist.*, 400 F. Supp.2d 707, 708 (2005).

51. Ibid. at 718.

52. Ibid.

53. Ibid.

54. Ibid. at 718.

55. Ibid. at 739.

56. Ibid.

57. Ibid.

58. Ibid.

59. Ibid.

60. Ibid. at 740.

61. Ibid. at 743.

62. Ibid. at 718.

63. Ibid. at 722.

64. Ibid.

65. Ibid. at 726. The judge relied in part on testimony from experts such as the distinguished scholar John F. Haught. Ibid. at 735. (Haught is the author of *Science and Religion: From Conflict to Conversation* [1995].)

66. Ibid. at 717.

67. Ibid. at 738.

68. Ibid. at 748, 752.

69. Ibid. at 719.

70. Ibid. at 765.

71. Ibid.

72. Laurie Goodstein, "A Decisive Election in a Town Roiled over Intelligent Design," *New York Times*, Nov. 10, 2005, A24; Jill Lawrence, "'Intelligent Design' Backers Lose in Pa.," *USA Today*, Nov. 10, 2005, A04.

73. Michael Shermer, *Why Darwin Matters: The Case against Intelligent Design*, 56 (2006); Arthur Peacocke, *Creation and the World of Science*, 78, 132 (1979).

74. Scott Atran, *Unintelligent Design*, in *Intelligent Thought: Science versus the Intelligent Design Movement* (John Brockman ed., 2006).

75. Henry Morris, "Intelligent Design and/or Scientific Creationism," http://www. icr .org/article/2708 (last visited Aug. 7, 2006).

76. In the words of a leading researcher, the "two foundational pillars upon which modern physics rests" are general relativity and quantum mechanics, yet "[a]s they are currently formulated, general relativity and quantum mechanics *cannot both be right.*" Brian Greene, *The Elegant Universe: Superstrings, Hidden Dimensions, and the Quest for the Ultimate Theory*, 3 (1999) (emphasis in the original).

77. An earlier version of my views on the importance of human origins to both sides of the evolution debate appears in Steven Goldberg, "Kennewick Man and the Meaning of Life," *University of Chicago Legal Forum* (2006): 301.

78. Ron Carlson and Ed Decker, *Fast Facts on False Teachings*, 62 (1994).

79. Ibid., 63.

80. Edward J. Larson, *Trial and Error: The American Controversy over Creation and Evolution*, 211 (2003).

81. Although Darrow described himself as an agnostic, he was usually viewed as an atheist. See *Closing Arguments: Clarence Darrow on Religion, Law, and Society*, xiii (S. T. Joshi ed., 2005).

82. Edward O. Wilson, *The Future of Life*, 133 (2002).

83. See, e.g., Stephen Jay Gould, *Wonderful Life: The Burgess Shale and the Nature of History*, 28 (1989). The way many scientists have identified evolution with progress from before Darwin to the present day is a theme of Michael Ruse, *The Evolution-Creation Struggle* (2005).

84. *Epperson* 393 U.S. 97, 111 (Black, J., concurring).

85. Ibid. at 116 (Stewart, J., concurring).

86. In 2000, some 31.4 percent of public high school graduates took a physics course; 91.2 percent took a biology course. See National Center for Education Statistics, *Digest of Education Statistics*, table 139 (2003), http://nces.ed.gov/programs/distes/do3/tables/dt139.asp (last visited Aug. 8, 2006).

87. See, e.g., Susan Kinzie, "Star of Physics Will Tell How Science Is Fun; Nobel Laureate Hopes His Stories Will Spark Interest in High School Students," *Washington Post Southern Maryland Extra* (Apr. 15, 2004), T03 (reporting on Leon Lederman's argument that "high school science is stuck in a time warp, a backward construction that begins with biology, proceeds to chemistry and eventually . . . gets to physics. But physics helps explain the basics of chemistry, and understanding chemistry is essential to understanding biology"); see also Leon Lederman, "Revolution in Science Education: Put Physics First!" *Physics Today* 54 (2001): 11 (arguing that physics should be taught before chemistry and biology).

88. For one of the relatively rare religious attacks on physics, see Donald R. Morse, "Big Bang or Big Collision: Where Does God Fit In?" *Journal of Religion & Psychical Research* 24 (2001): 121–22 (arguing that the Big Bang theory is flawed because of its omission of an intelligent God).

89. *Selman v. Cobb County Sch. Dist.*, 449 F.3d 1320 (11th Cir. 2006).

90. *Selman v. Cobb County Sch. Dist.*, 390 F. Supp.2d 1286, 1313 (N.D. Ga. 2005).

91. *Selman*, 449 F.3d 1320 (11th Cir. 2006).

92. Sir Francis Galton, *Inquiries into Human Faculty and Its Development* (1883); Richard Hofstadter, *Social Darwinism in American Thought* (1955); Kenneth M. Ludmerer, "The American Eugenics Movement: 1905–1930," in *Genetics in American Society: A Historical Appraisal* (Kenneth M. Ludmerer ed., 1972).

93. Ludmerer, "American Eugenics Movement," xx.

94. Ibid.; Gotz Aly, Peter Chroust, and Christian Pross, *Cleansing the Fatherland: Nazi Medicine and Racial Hygiene* (Belinda Cooper trans., 1994); Robert Jay Lifton, *The Nazi Doctors: Medical Killing and the Psychology of Genocide* (2000); Mark H. Haller, *Eugenics: Hereditarian Attitudes in American Thought*, 130–41 (1984).

95. Edward J. Larson, *Summer for the Gods: The Scopes Trial and America's Continuing Debate over Science and Religion*, 115 (1997); Willard H. Smith, "William Jennings Bryan and the Social Gospel," *Journal of American History* 53 (1966): 41, 59.

96. David A. DeWitt, "The Dark Side of Evolution," http://www.answersingenesis. org/docs2002/0510eugenics.asp (last visited Oct. 30, 2006); Tom DeRosa, "Fatal Fruit: From Darwin's Theory to Hitler's Holocaust," http://www.coralridge.org/darwin/legacy. asp?ID=crm&ec=I1301 (last visited Oct. 30, 2006).

97. Larson, *Summer for the Gods*, 191.

98. Ibid.

99. Ibid., 198–99.

100. See generally, Stephen J. Gould, *Rocks of Ages: Science and Religion in the Fullness of Life* (1999).

101. I discussed this point in Goldberg, *Seduced by Science*, 118–20.

102. William Jennings Bryan, "Closing Speech," www.law.umkc.edu/faculty/ projects/ftrials/scopes/bs.htm (last visited Oct. 31, 2006).

103. Saint Thomas Aquinas, *The Summa Theologica*, 1:v (Daniel J. Sullivan ed., 1977) (orig. pub. 1952).

104. Ibid., 12.

105. Ibid., 13.

106. Keith Thomson, *Before Darwin*, 5 (2005).

107. Ibid., 10.

108. Ibid.

109. Ibid., 6.

110. See, e.g., Thomas Nagel, "The Fear of Religion," *The New Republic* (Oct. 23, 2006), 25 (discussing Richard Dawkins, *The God Delusion* [2006]).

111. Indeed, Paley's *Natural Theology* does not even mention the Bible. Thomson, *Before Darwin*, 10.

112. Gerald Holton, "Einstein's Third Paradise," *Daedalus* 132 (Fall 2003): 26.

113. Ibid.

114. Dan Falk, *Universe on a T-Shirt: The Quest for the Theory of Everything*, 198 (2002).

115. Greene, *Elegant Universe*, 107.

116. Falk, *Universe on a T-Shirt*, 207.

117. See Richard Dawkins, *The God Delusion* (2006). On Dawkins's atheism, see ibid., 13 ("[Goodenough] is really as staunch an atheist as I am").

118. Ibid., 19. Dawkins adds, "[T]he reservation that 'cannot grasp' does not have to mean 'forever ungraspable.'" Ibid.

119. Margaret Gullan-Whur, *Within Reason: A Life of Spinoza*, 119–20 (1998).

120. Niels Bohr, "Discussion with Einstein: On Epistemological Problems," in *Atomic Physics in Albert Einstein: Philosopher-Scientist*, 210, 236–37 (Paul Arthur Schilpp ed., 1959).

121. This is, needless to say, an oversimplification of a complex matter. See generally, Stuart Hampshire, *Spinoza*, 39–50 (1973).

122. Ibid., 61–62, 121, 168–71.

123. Letter from Spinoza to Hugo Boxel 60(56) (undated), http://home.earthlink.net/~tneff/let6056.htm (last visited Nov. 7, 2006).

124. Steven Nadler, *Spinoza: A Life*, 231–32 (1999).

125. Ibid., 116–54.

126. Gullan-Whur, *Within Reason*, 304–7 (1998).

127. Allan Nadler, "Romancing Spinoza," *Commentary* (Dec. 2006): 25, 27.

128. Antonio Damasio, *Looking for Spinoza: Joy, Sorrow, and the Feeling Brain* (2003).

129. Greene, *Elegant Universe*, 3, 107.

130. Ibid., 4–20.

131. Falk, *Universe on a T-Shirt*, 173–74.

132. Lisa Randall, *Warped Passages: Unraveling the Mysteries of the Universe's Hidden Dimensions*, 458 (2005).

133. Greene, *Elegant Universe*, 386,

CHAPTER 4

1. I set forth an earlier version of some of these concerns in Goldberg, *Seduced by Science*, 92–97 (1999).

2. *Lynch v. Donnelly*, 465 U.S. 668 (1984).

3. Ibid. at 671.

4. Ibid.

5. Ibid. at 681.

6. Ibid. at 685.

7. Ibid. at 692.

8. Ibid.

9. Ibid. at 704.

10. "Permissible, If Slightly Profane," *New York Times*, Mar. 8, 1984, A22.

11. Ari L. Goldman, "Reaction Is Mixed on Nativity Ruling," *New York Times*, Mar. 7, 1984, A11.

12. *American Civil Liberties Union v. Birmingham*, 791 F.2d 1581, 1569 (6th Cir.) (Nelson, J., dissenting), cert. denied, 479 U.S. 939 (1986).

13. *American Jewish Congress v. City of Chicago*, 827 F.2d 120, 129 (7th Cir. 1987) (Easterbrook, J., dissenting).

14. *County of Allegheny v. American Civil Liberties Union*, 492 U.S. 573, 574–75 (1989).

15. Ibid. at 576.
16. Ibid. at 664 (Kennedy, J., concurring in part and dissenting in part).
17. Ibid. at 665–67.
18. Ibid. at 663–65.
19. Ibid. at 666.
20. Ibid. at 661, 664 n. 3.
21. Ibid. at 650 (Stevens, J., concurring in the judgment in part and dissenting in part).
22. Ibid. at 651–54.
23. Ibid. at 652–53.
24. Ibid. at 634 (O'Connor, J., concurring in part and concurring in the judgment).
25. Ibid. at 623.
26. Boris Fishman, "That Tree by the Menorah," *New York Times*, Dec. 19, 2004, 10.
27. Anthony Weiss, "Vandals Target Synagogue, Public Hanukkah Displays," *Forward*, Dec. 30, 2005, 5.
28. *King v. Village of Waunakee*, 517 N.W.2d 671, 673 (Wis. 1994).
29. Ibid.
30. Ibid. at 675.
31. Ibid. at 680.
32. Ibid. at 681.
33. Ibid. at 685 (Heffernan, C. J., dissenting).
34. Ibid. at 686.
35. Ibid. at 686–87.
36. Ibid. at 687.
37. *American Civil Liberties Union of New Jersey v. Schundler*, 104 F.3d 1435, 1438 (3d Cir. 1997).
38. Ibid.
39. *American Civil Liberties Union of New Jersey v. Schundler*, 931 F. Supp. 1180, 1181 (D.N.J. 1995).
40. *Schundler*, 104 F.3d at 1439.
41. Ibid. at 1450.
42. Ibid.
43. Ibid. at 1452.
44. Ibid.
45. Ibid. at 1452–53.
46. *American Civil Liberties Union of New Jersey v. Schundler*, 104 F.3d 1435 (3d Cir. 1997), cert. denied, 520 U.S. 1265 (1997). For a description of the subsequent litigation in this case, which resulted in a Third Circuit decision in favor of the Jersey City display, see Gabriel Acri, "*American Civil Liberties Union of New Jersey v. Schundler*: Established Endorsement in Need of 'Supreme' Intervention," *Catholic Law* 40 (2000): 165. The initial round of litigation is ably discussed in Laura Ahn, Case Note, "This Is Not a Crèche," *Yale Law Journal* 107 (1998): 1969.

47. B. Jessie Hill, "Putting Religious Symbolism in Context," *Michigan Law Review* 104 (2005): 491, 492.

48. *American Civil Liberties Union of New Jersey v. Schundler*, 168 F.3d 92 (3d Cir. 1999).

49. Ibid.

50. *Capitol Square Review Board v. Pinette*, 515 U.S. 753 (1995).

51. Ronald D. Rotunda and John E. Nowak, *Treatise on Constitutional Law: Substance and Procedure*, vol. IV, § 20.45 (3d ed. 1999).

52. *Cantwell v. Connecticut*, 310 U.S. 296 (1940); *Pinette* at 760. An earlier discussion of mine concerning these matters appears in Goldberg, *Seduced by Science*, 60–62.

53. John Michael Roberts, "The Enigma of Free Speech: Speakers' Corner, the Geography of Governance and a Crisis of Rationality," *Social & Legal Studies* 9 (2000): 271, 273.

54. "The Royal Parks, Hyde Park," www.royalparks.org.uk/tourists/index.cfm (last visited Nov. 7, 2006).

55. *Widmar v. Vincent*, 454 U.S. 263 (1981).

56. Ibid. at 278.

57. Ibid. at 272–73.

58. *Lamb's Chapel v. Center Moriches Union Free School Dist.*, 508 U.S. 34 (1993).

59. *Good News Club v. Milford Central School*, 533 U.S. 98 (2001).

60. Ibid. at 103.

61. Ibid. at 130–45.

62. *Pinette* at 757.

63. Ibid.

64. Ibid. at 818 n. 2.

65. Ibid. at 763.

66. Ibid. at 764–66.

67. Ibid. at 762.

68. Ibid. at 782 (O'Connor, J., concurring in part and concurring in the judgment); ibid. at 793–94 (Souter, J., concurring in part and concurring in the judgment).

69. Ibid. at 766 (majority opinion).

70. Ibid. at 818 (Ginsburg, J., dissenting).

71. *R.A.V. v. City of St. Paul, Minn.*, 505 U.S. 377, 392 (1992).

72. *Pinette* at 757–60.

73. Ibid. at 797 (Stevens, J., dissenting).

74. Ibid. at 770 (Thomas, J., concurring).

75. The origins of Chanukah and the nature of Chanukah observances are described in books such as Philip Goodman, *The Hanukkah Anthology* (1976), and Theodor Herzl Gaster, *Purim and Hanukah in Custom and Tradition: Feast of Lots, Feast of Lights* (1950).

76. Herman Wouk, *This Is My God: The Jewish Way of Life*, 84–90 (1988).

77. Ibid.

78. "Bringing Light to the Darkest of Seasons—a Chanukah How-To," *Jewish Exponent*, Dec. 18, 1997, 49.

79. Lawrence Bush and Jeffrey Dekro, "From Gelt to Tzedakah," *Tikkun*, Nov./ Dec. 2000, 49.

80. *The Jewish Encyclopedia* (1964), s.v. "Hanukkah."

81. "Bringing Light."

82. Julia Lieblich, "Hanukkah Links U.S. Jews to History, Heritage," *Chicago Tribune*, Nov. 29, 2002, 1.

83. David J. Goldberg and John D. Rayner, *The Jewish People: Their History and Their Religion*, 63–66 (1987).

84. Joseph Felser, "From Darkness to Light: A Philosophical Musing on the Hanukkah Myth, the Return of the Goddess, and the End of Religion," *Mythosphere* 1 (1999): 463.

85. *Encyclopaedia Judaica* (1972), s.v. "Hanukkah."

86. *Jewish Encyclopedia* (1964), s.v. "Torah."

87. *The New Encyclopedia of Judaism* (2002), s.v. "Hanukkah."

88. *The Jewish Encyclopedia* (1964), s.v. "Hanukkah."

89. Goodman, *Hanukkah Anthology*, 21.

90. Randi Barocas, "Holiday of Miracles: Traditions Notwithstanding, Jewish Survival Is Real Story behind Hanukkah," *Jewish News of Greater Phoenix*, Dec. 19, 1997, 10; Adin Steinsaltz, *The Essential Talmud*, 3 (1976).

91. See "The Lights of Chanukah—Laws and Customs," http://www.ou.org/chagim/ chanukah/somelaws.htm (last visited Nov. 10, 2006) (describing the dispute between Hillel and Shammai, as recounted in the Talmud in Masechet Shabbat 21b).

92. For the history and role of the seven-branched menorah, see Rachel Hachlili, *The Menorah, the Ancient Seven-Armed Candelabrum: Origin, Form and Significance* (2001), and Leon Yarden, *The Tree of Light: A Study of the Menorah, the Seven-Branched Lampstand* (1971).

93. *The Jewish Encyclopedia* (1964), s.v. "Temple of Herod."

94. Hans Dieter Betz, "Jesus and the Purity of the Temple (Mark 11:15–18): A Comparative Religion Approach," *Journal of Biblical Literature* 116 (1997): 455.

95. *Encyclopaedia Judaica* (1972), s.v. "Menorah."

96. Michael Kotzin, "Facing the Unresolved Issue in Interfaith Dialogue," *Forward*, Oct. 28, 2005, 11.

97. Ibid.

98. Ibid.

99. *Encyclopaedia Judaica* (1972), s.v. "Menorah."

100. *The Oxford Dictionary of the Jewish Religion* (1997), s.v. "Menorah."

101. Ibid.

102. *Oxford Dictionary of the Jewish Religion* (1997), s.v. "Magen David."

103. "Herman Wouk to Be Honored by Sharre Zedek," *Jerusalem Post*, Sept. 28, 1994, 12.

104. Natalie Gittelson, "American Jews Rediscover Orthodoxy," *New York Times* magazine, Sept. 30, 1984, 41.

105. Wouk, *This Is My God*, 87.

106. Ibid.

107. Ibid., 88.

108. Ibid., 90.

109. Jack Wertheimer, "Jews and the Jewish Birthrate," *Commentary*, Oct. 2005, 39.

110. Stephen Nissenbaum, *The Battle for Christmas*, 4 (1996).

111. Ibid.

112. Ibid.

113. William B. Waits, *The Modern Christmas in America*, 11 (1993).

114. Penne L. Restad, *Christmas in America*, 45 (1995).

115. Nissenbaum, *Battle for Christmas*, 261–64.

116. Ibid., 195–96.

117. Ibid., 6–7.

118. Ibid., 59–62.

119. Restad, *Christmas in America*, 61–64.

120. Nissenbaum, *Battle for Christmas*, 135.

121. Ibid., 134.

122. Restad, *Christmas in America*, 131.

123. Waits, *Modern Christmas in America*, 71.

124. Bill McKibben, *Hundred Dollar Holiday: The Case for a More Joyful Christmas*, 12 (1998).

125. John Gibson, *The War on Christmas: How the Liberal Plot to Ban the Sacred Christian Holiday Is Worse Than You Thought*, ix–xi (2005).

126. Ibid., xi.

127. Ibid.

128. Ibid., xix.

129. Pamela Miller, "'Happy Holidays' Doesn't Make Some Shoppers Very Merry," *Minneapolis–St. Paul Star Tribune*, Dec. 11, 2005, 1A.

130. Joe Garofoli, "Falwell Fighting for Holy Holiday; He'll Sue, Boycott Groups He Sees As Muzzling Christmas," *San Francisco Chronicle*, Nov. 20, 2005, A1.

131. Alana Semuels, "Wal-Mart Brings Christmas Back into Stores," *Los Angeles Times*, Nov. 10, 2006, C1.

132. Bassam Za'za, "OIC Urged to Resolve Cartoon Issue," *Gulf Times*, Feb. 3, 2006.

133. U.S. State Department, "United Arab Emirates International Freedom Report 2004" (Sept. 15, 2004), http://www.state.gov/g/drl/rls/irf/2004/35510.htm (last visited Nov. 10, 2006).

134. Simon Elegant, "The War for China's Soul," *Time*, Aug. 28, 2006, 40.

CHAPTER 5

1. Melissa Demiguel, "Christmas in France," http://www.bellaonline.com/articles/art38735.asp (last visited Aug. 29, 2006).

2. See, e.g., Noelle Knox, "Religion Takes a Back Seat in Western Europe," *USA Today*, Aug. 11, 2005, 1A.

3. U.S. Central Intelligence Agency, *World Factbook*, 197, 584 (2006).

4. Elaine Sciolino, "France Has a State Religion: Secularism," *New York Times*, Feb. 8, 2004, WK4.

5. "World Values Survey," www.worldvaluessurvey.org; www.jdsurvey.net/bdasepjds/ QuestionsMarginals.jsp (last visited Feb. 23, 2006).

6. Ibid.

7. Ibid.

8. U.S. Department of State, *Country Report on Human Rights Practices: Iran 1807–09*, vol. 2 (2004).

9. Ibid.; Quanuni Assassi Jumhuri'i Isla'mai Iran [The Constitution of the Islamic Republic of Iran] (1980).

10. Iran, "Human Rights Developments," *Human Rights Watch World Report* (1990): 441.

11. Code de l'éducation art. L. 141-5-1 (Fr.).

12. Elaine Sciolino, "France Turns to Tough Policy on Students' Religious Garb," *New York Times*, Oct. 22, 2004, A3.

13. As discussed later, this is established by statutory policy and by decisions such as *Chalifoux v. New Caney Independent School District*, 976 F. Supp. 659 (S.D. Tex. 1997).

14. The Free Exercise Clause was applied to the states in *Cantwell v. Connecticut*, 310 U.S. 296 (1940); the Establishment Clause was so applied in *Everson v. Board of Education*, 330 U.S. 1 (1947).

15. Richard S. Patterson and Richardson Dougall, *The Eagle and the Shield: A History of the Great Seal of the United States*, 83–84 (1976).

16. Anson Phelps Stokes and Leo Pfeffer, *Church and State in the United States*, 568 (rev. ed., 1964).

17. *Act of July 11, 1955*, Public Law 84-140, 69 Statutes 290 (1955) (codified at 31 U.S.C. § 5114 [2000]).

18. *Act of July 31, 1956*, Public Law 84-851, 70 Statutes 732 (codified as amended at 36 U.S.C. § 302 [2000]).

19. See, e.g., *Gaylor v. United States*, 74 F.3d 214 (10th Cir. 1996), cert. denied, 517 U.S. 1211 (1996).

20. Stokes and Pfeffer, *Church and State*, 569 (quoting President Theodore Roosevelt).

21. The pledge was upheld in *Sherman v. Community Consolidated School District 21 of Wheeling Township*, 980 F.2d 437 (7th Cir. 1992). The later decision, which the Supreme Court set aside, was *Newdow v. U.S. Congress*, 292 F.3d 597 (9th Cir. 2002), modified, 328 F.3d 466 (9th Cir. 2003), revised on other grounds sub nom. *Elk Grove Unified School Dist. v. Newdow*, 542 U.S. 1 (2004). This decision is discussed later.

22. *West Virginia State Board of Education v. Barnette*, 319 U.S. 624 (1943), discussed in Chapter 2.

23. See, e.g., *Engel v. Vitale*, 370 U.S. 421 (1962); *Abington School District v. Schempp*, 374 U.S. 203 (1963).

24. See, e.g., *Lee v. Weisman*, 505 U.S. 577 (1992). Lee left open the possibility of student-initiated prayer in public schools. For a discussion of this development coupled with a strong argument that such observances can lead to discrimination against religious minorities, see Frank S. Ravitch, *School Prayer and Discrimination: The Civil Rights of Religious Minorities and Dissenters* (1999).

25. *Elk Grove* at 6 (2004) (quoting J. Baer, *The Pledge of Allegiance: A Centennial History*, 1892–1992, 3 [1992]).

26. Ibid.

27. Ibid. at 25 (quoting H.R. Rep. No. 2047, 1 [1942]; S. Rep. No. 1477, 1 [1942]).

28. Ibid. at 7.

29. 100 *Cong. Rec.* 1700 (1954) (statement of Rep. Rabaut).

30. *Elk Grove* at 17.

31. Ibid. at 26, 31 (Rehnquist, C. J., concurring).

32. Ibid. at 45 (Thomas, J., concurring).

33. Ibid. at 6 (majority opinion).

34. Peter L. Berger, *Religion in a Revolutionary Society, in America's Continuing Revolution: An Act of Conservation*, 143 (Irving Kristol ed., 1975). It is not clear whether Eisenhower actually made this statement. See Richard John Neuhaus, "Who Needs God," *National Review*, Nov. 10, 1989, 52.

35. For an argument that free speech protection for religious activities is virtually identical to that provided by the free exercise doctrine, see Mark Tushnet, "The Redundant Free Exercise Clause?" *Loyola University Chicago Law Journal* 33 (2001): 71.

36. See, e.g., Stephen L. Carter, *God's Name in Vain: The Wrongs and Rights of Religion in Politics*, 20, 43–44 (2000). Carter's book presents an elegant argument that religious leaders should contribute to debates about public policy while avoiding partisan entanglements. In an important earlier work, Carter cautioned against trivializing religion by engaging in preaching that is too partisan. Stephen L. Carter, *The Culture of Disbelief: How American Law and Politics Trivialize Religious Devotion*, 70 (1993). For a subtle critique of Carter's approach, see Leslie Griffin, "Review Essay: The Trivialization of Religion," *Wisconsin Law Review* 1994 (1995): 1287.

37. There is a lively scholarly debate over the prudence (as contrasted with the legality) of introducing religious arguments into public debate. I have discussed elsewhere the writings of scholars such as Kent Greenawalt, John Rawls, and Michael Perry on this issue, and I set forth there my belief that "in the vast majority of cases . . . there is no real problem with presenting religious views in [such debate]; in fact, important values are served when those views are aired." Goldberg, *Seduced by Science*, 130 (1999). Substantive religious arguments in favor of policies that also serve secular ends are far removed from the empty symbols that concern me here.

38. *Pierce v. Society of Sisters*, 268 U.S. 510 (1925).

39. Ibid.

40. See, e.g., Stephen G. Gilles, "On Educating Children: A Parentalist Manifesto," *University of Chicago Law Review* 63 (1996): 937, 987–88.

41. *Pierce* at 534; *Murphy v. State of Arkansas*, 852 F.2d 1039, 1043 (8th Cir. 1988); Stephen P. Broughman and Nancy L. Swaim, *Characteristics of Private Schools in the United States: Results from the 2003–2004 Private School Universe Survey*, table 3 (2006); Gregory J. Cizek, "Religious Education in Home Schools: Goals/Outcomes Mismatch?" *Religious Education* 89 (1994): 43, 44.

42. Broughman and Swaim, *Characteristics of Private Schools*, table 3 (2006); Cizek, "Religious Education in Home Schools," 43, 44.

43. There are 5,122,772 students in private schools across the United States, of whom 4,200,779 attend religious schools. Broughman and Swaim, *Characteristics of Private Schools*, table 12.

44. *Zelman v. Simmons-Harris*, 536 U.S. 639, 653 (2002).

45. Ibid. at 662.

46. *United States v. Ballard*, 322 U.S. 78, 81 (1944).

47. Ibid. at 82–83.

48. Ibid. at 86–87.

49. *Church of the Lukumi Babalu Aye, Inc. v. City of Hialeah*, 508 U.S. 520, 524 (1993).

50. *Employment Div., Dept. of Human Resources of Oregon v. Smith*, 494 U.S. 872, 876 (1990).

51. Ibid. at 877–78.

52. 42 U.S.C. § 1996a(b)(1) (2000) provides: "Notwithstanding any other provision of law, the use, possession, or transportation of peyote by an Indian for bona fide traditional ceremonial purposes in connection with the practice of a traditional Indian religion is lawful, and shall not be prohibited by the United States or any State." 42 U.S.C. § 1996a(a)(3) notes that twenty-eight states have enacted laws protecting ceremonial use of peyote by Indian religious practitioners.

53. Religious Freedom Restoration Act of 1993, 42 U.S.C. § 2000bb (2000).

54. *Gonzales v. O Centro Espiríta Beneficiente União do Vegetal*, 126 S. Ct. 1211 (2006).

55. Ibid. at 1217.

56. Ibid.

57. Ibid. at 1220 (quoting 21 U.S.C. § 812[b][1] [2000]).

58. Ibid. at 1216.

59. Ibid. The *O Centro* case also involved a treaty, which is beyond the scope of our discussion.

60. Ibid. at 1218.

61. Ibid. at 1220.

62. Ibid. at 1218.

63. Ibid. at 1223.

64. *City of Boerne v. Flores*, 521 U.S. 507 (1997).

65. James A. Hanson, "Missouri's Religious Freedom Restoration Act: A New Approach to the Cause of Conscience," *Missouri Law Review* 69 (2004): 853, 862 n. 53; Alabama Constitution amend no. 622; *Arizona Revised Statutes Annotated* § 41-1493.01 (West 2004); *Connecticut General Statutes Annotated* § 52-571b (West 2005); *Florida Statutes Annotated* § 761.01-.05 (West 2005); *Idaho Code* § 73-402 (Michie 2006); 775 *Illinois Compiled Statutes* 35/15 (Supp. 2006); *Missouri Annotated Statutes* § 1.302 (West Supp. 2006); *New Mexico Statutes Annotated* § 28-22-3 (Michie 2006); *Oklahoma Statutes Annotated* tit. 51, § 251–58 (West Supp. 2006); *Rhode Island General Laws* § 42-80.1-3 (1998); *South Carolina Code Annotated* § 1-32-40 (Law. Co-op. 2005); *Texas Civil Practice & Remedies Code Annotated* § 110.003 (Vernon 2005).

66. *Walz v. Tax Comm'n of City of New York*, 397 U.S. 664, 668–69 (1970).

67. *Cutter v. Wilkinson*, 544 U.S. 709, 720 (2005). For a strongly critical account of many of the accommodations legislatures have fashioned for religious practice, see Marci A. Hamilton, *God vs. the Gavel: Religion and the Rule of Law* (2005).

68. I have made this point in Steven Goldberg, "Cutter and the Preferred Position of the Free Exercise Clause," *William & Mary Bill of Rights Journal* 14 (2006): 1403.

69. *U.S. v. Seeger*, 380 U.S. 163 (1965); *Welsh v. U.S.*, 398 U.S. 333 (1970).

70. *Wisconsin v. Yoder*, 406 U.S. 205, 216 (1972).

71. *Torcaso v. Watkins*, 367 U.S. 488, 495 (1961).

72. Ibid. at 495 n. 11.

73. Ibid.

74. *Fellowship of Humanity v. County of Alameda*, 315 P.2d 394 (Cal. Ct. App. 1957).

75. Ibid. at 397.

76. I have argued this point in Goldberg, *Seduced by Science*.

77. *Malnak v. Yogi*, 592 F.2d 197 (3d Cir. 1979).

78. Ibid. at 198.

79. Ibid.

80. Ibid. at 198 and n. 2.

81. *Malnak v. Yogi*, 440 F. Supp. 1284, 1310 (D.N.J. 1977).

82. *Malnak*, 592 F.2d at 200.

83. Ibid. (Adams, J., concurring).

84. *Africa v. Com. of Pa.*, 662 F.2d 1025 (3d Cir. 1981); *Grove v. Mead School Dist. No. 354*, 753 F.2d 1528 (9th Cir. 1985); *New Creation Fellowship of Buffalo v. Town of Cheektowaga, N.Y.*, No. 99-CV-460A(F), 2004 WL 1498190 (W.D.N.Y. Jul. 2, 2004).

85. *Malnak*, 592 F.2d at 208 (Adams, J., concurring).

86. Ibid. at 209.

87. Ibid.

88. Ibid.

89. Ibid.

90. Ibid. at 208.

91. Ibid. at 213.

92. Ibid.

93. Ibid. at 214.

94. Ibid. at 208.

95. *Corporation of the Presiding Bishop of the Church of Jesus Christ of Latter-Day Saints v. Amos*, 483 U.S. 327 (1987).

96. *Civil Rights Act of 1964* § 703 (42 U.S.C. § 2000e-2 [2000]).

97. Ibid., § 702.

98. *Amos* at 332 n. 9.

99. Ibid.

100. Ibid. at 330.

101. Ibid. at 331.

102. Ibid. at 335, 338.

103. *Locke v. Davey*, 540 U.S. 712, 715 (2004).

104. Ibid. at 716.

105. Ibid. at 718.

106. Ibid. at 715.

107. Ibid. at 719.

108. Ibid. at 722–23.

109. *Cutter v. Wilkinson*, 544 U.S. 709, 712 (2005).

110. Brief for Respondents at 13–15, *Cutter v. Wilkinson*, 544 U.S. 709 (2005) (No. 03-9877).

111. *Cutter* at 722–23.

112. *Locke* at 718 (quoting *Walz v. Tax Comm'n of City of New York*, 397 U.S. 664, 669 [1970]).

113. Michael S. Ariens and Robert A. Destro, *Religious Liberty in a Pluralistic Society*, 550 (2d ed., 2002) (discussing *Attorney General v. Pearson* [1817]).

114. Ibid.

115. *Jones v. Wolf*, 443 U.S. 595 (1979).

116. Exhibit, Joint App., 228, *Jones v. Wolf*, 443 U.S. 595 (1979) (No. 78-91); John W. Whitehead, "The Conservative Supreme Court and the Demise of the Free Exercise of Religion," *Temple Political and Civil Rights Law Review* 7 (1997): 1, 26.

117. *Wolf*, 443 U.S. at 598–99.

118. On the distinction between congregational and hierarchical churches, see *Watson v. Jones*, 80 U.S. 679 (1872).

119. *Jones v. Wolf*, 243 S.E.2d 860, 863 (Ga. 1978).

120. Ibid.

121. Ibid. at 864.

122. *Wolf*, 443 U.S. at 602.

123. Ibid.

124. Ibid. at 610–21 (Powell, J., dissenting).

125. Ibid. at 607–8 (majority opinion).

126. Ibid. at 603.

127. See generally, Ashley Alderman, Note, "Where's the Wall?: Church Property Disputes within the Civil Courts and the Need for Consistent Application of the Law," *Georgia Law Review* 39 (2005): 1027.

128. *Dixon v. Edwards*, 290 F.3d 699 (4th Cir. 2002).

129. Ibid. at 703.

130. Ibid.

131. Ibid. at 716.

132. Ibid. at 706 n. 8.

133. Ibid. at 714.

134. E. J. Dionne Jr., "In France, Scarves and Secularism," *Washington Post*, Dec. 23, 2003, A21 (Presidents Clinton and George W. Bush opposed the French approach).

135. Steve Barnes, "School District Settles Suit over Muslim Head Scarf," *New York Times*, May 20, 2004, A20.

136. Jay Cooper, "Teachers Told of Their Role in Ensuring Religious Rights," *Tulsa World*, Apr. 30, 2004, A20.

137. Ibid.

138. U.S. Department of Justice, Complaint-in-Intervention, *Hearn v. Muskogee Pub. Sch. Dist.*, C.A. No. 03-598-S, ¶ 1.13 (E.D. Okla., Mar. 2004), http://www.usdoj .gov/crt/religdisc/complaint-in-intervention2.pdf. (last visited Aug. 29, 2006).

139. *Oklahoma Statutes Annotated* tit. 51, § 253 (West Supp. 2006).

140. Consent Decree, *Hearn v. Muskogee Pub. Sch. Dist.*, C.A. No. 03-598-S (E.D. Okla., May 20, 2004), http://www.usdoj.gov/crt/religdisc/hearn_consent_decree_final .pdf. (last visited Aug. 29, 2006).

141. *Chalifoux v. New Caney Independent School Dist.*, 976 F. Supp. 659, 663 (S.D. Tex. 1997).

142. Ibid. at 663.

143. Ibid. at 667.

144. *Cheema v. Thompson*, No. 94-16097, 1994 WL 477725 (9th Cir., Sep. 2, 1994), opinion withdrawn by *Cheema v. Thompson*, 67 F.3d 883 (9th Cir. 1995).

145. ACLU of Northern California, "Settlement Reached in Lawsuit Concerning Rights of Baptized Sikh Students to Wear Symbolic Ceremonial Knives to School," June 12, 1997, http://www.aclunc.org/news/press_releases/settlement_reached_in_lawsuit _concerning_rights_of_baptized_sikh_students_to_wear_symbolic_ceremonial_knives _to_school.shtml (last visited Sept. 26, 2007).

146. Alison Bert, "Sikh Student Allowed to Carry Small Religious Sword," Mar. 16, 1997, http://www.saldef.org/content.aspx?a=1089 (last visited Oct. 26, 2006).

147. Ibid.

148. Excerpted from Magna Carta clauses 1–54 (1215), http://www.nuli.ml/thingspll/ magnacarta/translation.html (last visited Oct. 26, 2006). For variant translations, see note 149.

149. On the history of the Magna Carta, see, e.g., Claire Breay, *Magna Carta: Manuscripts and Myths* (2002). For variations in the translations, compare ibid., 49, with Ray Stringham, *Magna Carta: Fountainhead of Freedom*, 227 (1966). For a discussion of the role of Jews and women in the world in which the Magna Carta was written, see Geoffrey Hindley, *The Book of Magna Carta*, 99–125 (1990).

150. See Christine N. Cimini, "Principles of Non-arbitrariness: Lawlessness in the Administration of Welfare," *Rutgers Law Review* 57 (2005): 451, 463–68.

151. For the idea of certain hormones governing love, see "I Get a Kick out of You: The Science of Love," *The Economist*, Feb. 14, 2004, 89.

152. E.g., *Reynolds v. United States*, 98 U.S. 145, 164 (1879).

153. Thomas Jefferson, *Notes on the State of Virginia*, 159–60 (William Peden ed., 1955). *Notes on the State of Virginia* first appeared in 1784.

154. Roger Williams, "Cotton's Letter Examined" (1644), reprinted in *Complete Writings of Roger Williams*, 1:313, 392 (Samuel L. Caldwell ed., 1963).

155. Noah Feldman, *Divided by God: America's Church-State Problem—and What We Should Do about It*, 256 n. 13 (2005). I am indebted to Feldman for this careful observation, which I had not seen elsewhere. His book contains many important

insights, and Feldman and I share a desire to "tone down" the "fevered pitch of debate" over church-state issues. Ibid., 16. Our primary difference is that Feldman believes that nonexclusionary religious displays and prayers should be allowed in the public sphere, in part because this can be done "without watering all of them down into a single nondenominational soup." Ibid., 242. I believe that so much watering down of religion would result from any legally and politically acceptable approach that the game is not worth the candlestick.

Bibliographic Note

A detailed bibliography for *Bleached Faith* can be found at the Stanford University Press website, www.sup.org.

Index